THIS BOOK IS BROUGHT TO YOU BY MY STUDENT LOANS

MEGAN J. KALEITA

CL◀SH

To Sean, because he won't let me give up.

CONTENTS

FOREWORD BY ANDREW SHAFFER

Think of the worst job you've ever had. Got it? Good. Now imagine a seven-year old girl, freezing in the late autumn air, dismembering a deer carcass with a bow-saw for her self-employed father's meat-packaging business. And now, if you can, imagine that same girl, a decade-and-a-half later, plunging the condom-clogged toilets at a no-tell motel while fending off advances from skeevy johns.

If you're not sufficiently horrified, imagine doing these things for little or no pay. Scary, right? Welcome to Megan Kaleita's world.

As I type these words, the unemployment rate is hovering near a 50-year low. Unfortunately, as far too many Americans in the workforce know—the majority of whom are millennials—statistics don't tell the full story. Many jobs these days are low-paying, part-time, and lacking meaningful benefits like health insurance.

"More than one-third of working millennials have more than one job," Kaleita writes. (That doesn't include so-called "side-hustles" like Uber, Etsy, or flipping Funko Pop chase variants on eBay.) To top it all off, a staggering 62% of millennials are saddled with $10,000 or more in student debt.

Kaleita's story is all too common: A long line of crap jobs, punctuated with a few stints in college, each degree promising a brighter future but instead just adding to the debt clinging to her back like a monkey. However, her background—she grew up in a rural, working-class community—gives her a welcome and refreshing perspective on the ups and downs of higher education and the fractured working-class economy.

Reporters and sociologists occasionally make headlines by going "undercover" in the working class economy, taking low-paying jobs and "trying to survive." The results are almost always (unintentionally) laughable. Kaleita doesn't need to go undercover to report from the front lines, though. She's been living there her entire life. There's a raw authenticity to her voice. Her writing is unpretentious yet inventive, riddled with a healthy dose of black humor.

You'll learn this fairly quickly, but it still must be said: Kaleita doesn't suffer fools lightly. This leads to friction with her co-workers, customers, and patients. She's too smart for her own good at times, equipped with a better working knowledge of fair labor acts and sex-based discrimination laws than her bosses.

If I were her manager, I would fire her on the spot after reading this book. Not because she's a lawsuit waiting to happen—she might be—but because *This Book Is Brought To You By My Student Loans* makes it clear the job she's most qualified for is being a writer.

THE BLIND WIZARD I MET AT MY HOSPITAL JOB

I was working outpatient registration at a small rural hospital when the wizard checked in. Despite what catastrophe-porn medical shows would have you believe, working in medicine becomes genuinely dull after a while. People don't come stumbling in the doors with some weird cancer, already half in love with their attending physician, and then die tragically after a 22 episode arc. They mostly come to hospitals because they have to get a routine test for something totally boring. In any case, the wizard came in for a routine blood test.

The wizard gave me the shivers. A few of my coworkers had dealt with him on and off and said he was a spooky fucker. He wasn't well known in town and he had a PO box but no physical address. In a small town where everybody knows where everybody else lives, not knowing where someone as spooky as the wizard lived just made him more enigmatic.

His eyes were a milky blue and my first thought when I looked into his weather-beaten face was that this guy was committing to his look with some expensive professional contact lenses. Then I realized he was blind, which was hard to believe.

When I called him into my office, he walked in a confident line across the waiting room without a guide dog, assistant, or cane; dodging wheelchairs and orderlies with nimble panache and a jolly smile.

He heaved his girth into the chair across from my desk. His beard was that of legends; he easily could have come in first in a beard contest that hosted Gimli, Gandalf, and Dumbledore. A large red stone hung around his neck and rested on his round stomach. From hearing about this guy, I expected your run of the mill new age eccentric. Someone who smelled like armpit and wore a howling wolf t-shirt and a pot steel pentagram, and watery sighted eyes that would probably stare at my tits the whole time.

Nope, not this guy.

His black cotton tunic had slightly belled sleeves with silver cufflinks in the shape of snakes. A large fat opal sat on his pinky like a sparkly egg, and he wore a hand-embroidered blue wool vest that spanned the continent of his shoulders. Everything this guy wore was bespoke and on anybody else would have screamed "*I Love Renaissance Faires!*" but looked exactly perfect on him. His black linen pants were obviously handmade and tucked in neatly to soft leather boots. His caregiver, a tall lanky woman with wild grey hair who stood quietly off to the side, wore a long black dress and a green velvet shawl, clasped closed at the shoulder with what looked like a high-quality reproduction of the Tara brooch.

I checked him in for routine outpatient blood work and advised him of our new laboratory policy: that any unused tissue or blood samples collected during routine procedures would be used to train student technicians. Our entire exchange to that point had been pretty jovial. I explained the facility policy for lab samples and I am not shitting you: the lights flickered.

"I won't allow it!" he boomed.

I hadn't been trained for this; the hospital administrators obviously couldn't think up a scenario where someone would have a problem with using leftover blood and tissue to train new technicians. I cobbled together the best response I could.

"Okay. I understand that this practice isn't in line with your faith —"

He cut me off, rising from the chair and breathing heavily.

"It is a danger to me! If mine enemies knew they could get my blood without my knowledge, I would be vulnerable to spiritual attacks!"

Before I could think of anything to say, he continued on even though his caregiver tried to calm him.

"You do not understand the danger you have put me in! I've let you beasts take my blood for your own cruel needs, to nourish your own hollow spirits! Nobody listens — my afflictions are spiritual, that's how I'm able to see! I will my spirit past my body and project myself outward and become my own spiritual eyes. I'm not being poisoned by sugar, I'm being poisoned by dark and ancient magics. I demand to know who you sold my spirit to!"

I wanted to say I sold mine and his to pay off Sallie Mae but I stayed quiet. His head whipped in my direction and I seriously believed for a second that he could read minds.

"There is a darkness hovering over you! The longer you stay with these beasts it will consume you!" That's pretty much how I felt about that job, so yeah.

He continued yelling at me like a Skyrim side quest

character until one of the administrative nurses was paged. She came into the small office with us and closed the door, giving the Wizard a smile, he couldn't see and a reassuring pat he flinched away from.

"Don't touch me, devil woman! I can see your aura is weak and you lack conviction of soul and substance!"

In all fairness, I kind of thought the same thing about the administrative nurse — Sue was a kind of a bitch.

Sue offered him an orange juice and that helped put him at ease. Spiritual affliction or not, he drank down that OJ like it was an elixir of great magic. They left my cubicle, he leaned in towards me and with his milky eyes fixed on my forehead, he breathed deeply.

I don't know what I expected him to say. I was hoping for something with the literary and fantastical impact of "They passed down all the roads long ago" or "make it so."

His breath rattled and he said, "just refund my copay to the PO box on file and I'm going to need another orange juice."

THE TIME I ALMOST SHIT MYSELF BECAUSE A CUSTOMER HAD TO ASK ME 1,000 QUESTIONS

The summer between my Junior and Senior year of college, I found myself working in the timeshare office of one of the last standing Catskill resorts; Morretto's Resort and Casino. Summers were a panicky time for me financially. I wanted to have fun but I also wanted to have some cash together so I wouldn't be flat on my ass and desperate by the time I graduated.

Double shifts at the local resort and casino made that possible. I had to wear a black tunic with a wide collar like a pilgrim with long grey palazzo pants that felt like they were made out of bathing suit material and we couldn't wear open-toed shoes in case we had "ugly feet." It mostly sucked, but it was my first summer job not cleaning toilets or babysitting, so I was mostly happy with it.

This resort, like many others, was family owned. The owner's niece was my boss and her daughter was one of my coworkers. My boss, Linda, had hired on a bunch of her daughter's friends for the day shift, all of whom called her "Mamma Love" and got paid at least $5 more an hour than the evening shift did. The day shift was comprised of my boss, her daughter, and her daughter's friends. The evening/overnight shift was me and three older ladies who had worked for the company for twenty years.

Even though there was crazy nepotism on the day shift and 90% of the work went undone, I got the better end of the stick. The ladies I worked with were a little sassy, a little mean, and a lot of fun to hang out with when the day started to slow down around 8pm.

We didn't call Linda "Mama Love" but Connie, my one coworker, did call her a twat to her face once.

The Fourth of July Weekend that year was also the grand reopening for some areas of the hotel so we were all put on double shifts. The day shift worked from 7 to 7 and the evening shift worked noon to midnight. When I got there at 11:45, traffic was backed up down the street so I had to park out in town and walk a quarter mile to the hotel.

I had my uniform on and my name tag proudly resting on my left boob as I walked past the line of cars. I hadn't even reached the actual resort to clock in and I had people rolling down their windows and asking for things. I got $50 in tips out of it, so I'm not totally annoyed at that experience. We also weren't supposed to accept tips, but if Patrick Swayze could live a good life in Dirty Dancing then I could make some extra bank in the Catskills.

* * *

In the early evening, the office was pandemonium. Not surprisingly, Mama Love and most of the day shift were "out sick." We were going to be shorthanded on the busiest weekend of the year. The concierge and the bellhops had started shuttling people from overflow parking two miles away to the resort's restaurants and bars so they could get nice and shit-faced before they checked in. It got money flowing and kept the lines shorter than they would normally be.

The kitchens sent a bellboy to our office with three big platters of food and some bottled water. We had ten minutes until the next shuttle of guests came hurtling at us, so we made sure we got time to pee and hydrate. The kitchen had sent us spaghetti and we scarfed it down too fast to notice that it tasted weird.

Thirty minutes later, my coworker, Lydia was checking in a large rowdy group because she was the best at wrangling drunks. She was a lovely lady in her early fifties who gave me advice about school, and hugs when I needed them. I liked her. She was checking in a particularly belligerent drunken guest when she held up a delicate finger to him, indicating she needed a moment, turned and gently vomited into the trash can next to her. The entire process was so polite that an alien coming to our planet would think it was a natural part of our customs.

The office cleared out pretty fast after that, most of the guests horrified and stunned, rubbing themselves with copious amounts of hand sanitizer and refusing anything we handed them. One woman asked me to just point out her keys to her and she grabbed them herself. It was like Mask of the Read Death in there.

We scooted Lydia out into the adjoining office near the trashcan and finished checking in the next carload of angry drunks. I was sweating through my uniform and my stomach felt like the Blob was hanging out between my ribcage and my colon. One look at Patty and Stacey and I could tell they were in the same boat. And it wasn't just sympathetic barfing: Connie was in the bathroom making splattery-exorcism sounds and I made peace with the fate of my ass and gag reflexes.

Connie, Lydia, Stacy and I were goners. There was only one unisex bathroom in our office but the next building over had several. Stacy was the first to get hit and ran across the parking lot to the maintenance building with a trash can.

I followed closely behind, checking my options. I actively considered shitting myself and then just jumping into the ornamental duck pond.

The legs of my gaucho uniform pants were so wide that I could probably pull one of them up around my butt and not get any poop on me. I was in that weird limbo where I wasn't sure if my underwear was soaked with sweat or an ill-trusted fart, so I had already written them off.

I dove into the maintenance building and shoved the few security guys out of the way and barreled to the bathroom. I had seen Stacy's fluffy ponytail whip around the other corner; that little bitch had opted to scurry past the first available bathroom because it was an office filled with dudes and had the acoustical qualities of the Sydney Opera House. I had no choice but to bolt the door and unleash a flood of the unspeakable. I could hear them cackling outside.

I leaned back with my head against the wall and wished for death. Not from embarrassment, or humiliation, because everybody poops. But from the hellfire cramps that ripped through me. When I thought I could stand, I finished up and went outside to face the ring of horrified maintenance guys.

If you're wondering, I was wrong about my underwear. Wrong but lucky.

* * *

I came back to an office that was unstaffed, full of guests, and smelled like barf. I almost checked the duck pond, figuring I'd find Connie or Lydia face down and covered in fecal ejecta and duckweed, moaning like the Toxic Avenger.

Patty came out of the bathroom looking pretty bad, but she had soaked the sweat off her face with a paper towel and put a little pressed-powder back on. It only made her look even worse. Together, between waves of nausea and colon shredding cramps, we checked in the guests and then collapsed behind the desk.

Stacey called me from the bathroom stall in the maintenance building and asked me to call her brother to pick her up. Lydia was on the floor in the manager's office, a wet paper towel on her eyes and an alarmingly full trash can next to her. Connie had just left.

"I'm not shitting myself for $8.50 an hour," had been her farewell cry as she hopped into her car.

A busy resort hotel is a weird thing. There are people everywhere and nowhere at the same time. It's basically Schroedinger's vacation.

Patty and I put an Out Of Order sign on the bathroom door so we could continue to use it for our own ungodly means without a guest being in the way. We divvied up the receipts and cash bags for the night in-between checking in guests and bouts of power shitting and projectile barfing.

We had been advised by the kitchen, about two hours too late, that they had accidentally given us food from a broken freezer. They had also given food poisoning to two of the bartenders and one security guard. Everybody was on stand-by to just try and cope until or if they could find replacements for us.

We were in the home stretch by about 8pm. Guests all usually headed for one of the seven bars on site and dumped their kids at the supervised playground after the dining halls closed. We only had five parties who hadn't checked in. I was shaking and sweating but I had found a loose Imodium in the bottom of my purse and swallowed it dry. I had hope.

But then a New Jersey soccer mom walked in.

She was concerned that her condo was butted up too close to the woods and wanted to move to a better one over-looking the lake. She had a Kate Gosselin haircut and was short and barrel-shaped. A large white gold crucifix took up most of the space of her chest that wasn't deeply wrinkled and bronzed cleavage. She had white gold bamboo hoops that dangled dangerously from her earlobes. Those fuckers had to be about two pounds per earlobe, I have no idea how she didn't knock herself out when she moved. Misery followed her like a cloud.

She waddled up to the desk.

"Can I help you?"

She looked me up and down and decided that whatever it was that made me look like shit was my own problem. But it was kind of her problem too because I was starting to get that sick person stomach bug smell. She wrinkled her nose and gave me *the stare*.

"We need to move condos. This one is too close to the woods. We'll get attacked by bears."

"I can assure you, condo 624 is buffered by an orna-mental strip of Japanese maples. Bears don't like those."

"Oh, great!" She threw her hands up in that exaggerated gesture that's supposed to make her rural inferiors cower. "There's fuckin' pandas out here!"

"There are no pandas out here."

"How do you know? There could be Japanese beetles! What if my dog eats one!" At this point I noticed that she had a small, scraggly white dog clamped tightly in her armpit. Its little-pointed face jutted out from under her arm, all wire haired and goggle-eyed. Jim Henson himself would have been jealous of this pairing.

Before I could respond, I had a feeling like a tube of toothpaste being squeezed in the middle with the cap still on. Something was going to come out of one or both ends and I wasn't going to have much say in the matter.

"Your family owns condo 624 for this timeshare week. It's a holiday week and unless there's an emergency, you know you can't get a refund or be relocated without reason," I said weakly. My knees shook and it felt like gasoline in my stomach. Sweat beaded down my back and my stomach clenched again.

"Are you sure there's no bears in the area?"

"Yes." No. I hope your whole fucking orange family gets eaten.

"What about mountain lions?"

"Nope."

"Should I be worried about ticks? I'm allergic to Lyme. "

"We can have some bug spray sent to your room from the concierge." Everyone is allergic to Lyme's disease you jack off, that's why it's a disease.

"Okay, yeah. Do that. Now listen, how come last spring it wasn't so muggy?"

"Global warming."

My breathing was uneven and I was barely holding on. A

slight breeze could have made me crap my pants. In a bizarre way, this woman torturing me had become my lifeline. I was locked into my position at the desk and if I so much as brushed a stray hair from my face, I would be on the first train to brown town. We were bound in fire and flame, by our souls, our needs, our wants. Our lives were entwined — this would be the woman I shit myself in front of and to her I would always be that hotel check girl who shit herself that one time. We were bound by our stories. There was no going back.

"I'm sorry you're concerned but we can book you first thing tomorrow with our timeshare reps. They can work with you to move you to another condo next year."

Sensing weakness, Jersey hesitated. I stood like a statue, a butt clenched marble statue. But Jersey didn't budge, while Patty was making little gulping noises of pre-puking. Jersey just eyed me up and down and then looked back at the brochure.

"Can I pick out the color of our condo with these new upgrades? 'Cause the one I'm in right now, the guest room is mauve and let me tell you I just can't make my sons sleep in a mauve room. They're boys!"

Patty made another wet gulping noise and scurried out the door. Jersey didn't bat an eye. I took in a shaky breath.

"The guest rooms are being done in royal blue. The master bedrooms are being done in hunter green. The bathrooms are a light yellow, and the kitchens are being done in country red."

"Ugh, country red. If I wanted a farmhouse I'd buy one, but I'm not piece-a-shit hillbilly. They should really get our input more often."

I realized then that my only choice was to shit my pants. I had been working at that resort for a month and I enjoyed it, but I was going to have to go out with a blaze of glory. It's like in movies when the hero knows they have to sacrifice themselves. Things just go a lot more smoothly when you accept your fate and embrace it, like a T-800 lowering itself into molten steel.

My whole body was in knots and I didn't even trust myself to make the five steps to the bathroom anyway. I had completely stopped listening to a word this woman was saying. She was paging through the brochure, bitching about the renovations and answering her own questions. She looked at me again.

"You don't look great."

"It's been a long day." And I have chosen to shit myself. I accepted that I was going to shit myself, much like others accept God or Jesus. I accepted that I have no control over my anus and that this was a sacrifice I must make.

She nodded and I had no idea if I said that last part out loud or not.

She might have smelled what just happened because she finally shut up, and grabbed an activities schedule and a few more brochures and meekly wished me a good night.

The moral of this story is to always put your butthole first and never let anybody make you put your personal discomfort on the back burner. And if they do, crapping yourself is a really effective way to make sure they never bother you again.

I AM TOTALLY NOT LYING ON THIS RESUME

Megan J. Kaleita

Look! My address is in a super-important looking font that I'm not going to use anywhere else in this letter!

Phone Number that could be shut off before you respond because I'm broke.

_____

Omg, look, it's a fancy line! I know how to make a fancy line, please hire me!

Greetings, Nancy of Human Resources!

This introduction paragraph is for getting your attention, so I stand out as a premiere applicant for a job I definitely need but do not want. Ready to pay attention to me and have your mind blown? I killed a man once.

My work experience in this field is just as dreary as it sounds but I'm going to spend this entire paragraph making it seem like learning how to administer Narcan during an active shooter drill has literally given me a huge professional, goal-oriented work boner. Honestly, learning how to do that may have lost me ten years off my life but I'm just going to make it sound like it was the best thing that ever happened to me and that it changed my perspective on life and my career goals. Now I'm all about learning new things, asking questions, promoting synergy, upward mobility, and not getting shot while saving someone from a potentially fatal overdose of heroin.

I'm proficient in both Apple and Microsoft platforms but that doesn't matter because your company is still using Microsoft XP and eventually you're going to call me into your office to help you change your desktop background to a picture of a wine glass on a beach wearing tiny sunglasses with the caption "It's Wine 'O'Clock Somewhere!" written in comic sans. After I do this you're going to think I'm after your job and resent the hell out of me, making my life harder than it needs to be.

I work well in a team setting or by myself, which is really bullshit because I hate working in teams because, to quote Sartre, "Hell is other people." Look at how educated I am! I bet you can't wait to pay me drastically less than a man with half my education is currently making. I can't wait either!

> Hire me or don't,
> Megan J. Kaleita

Resume Profile: Hey check it out! I used that same font again!

You're not going to read this at all so I'm not sure why the Harvard Business Review told me to write this paragraph since this job is in Nowhere, Ass Scratch where the next closest town is East BumblePiss Mountainside, which is still a three hour drive away with good snow tires. You're just happy there isn't any ketchup on this paper. This paragraph is just reiterating everything I put in my cover letter, only with more buzz words. Here's a good one: excellent Microsoft Excel skills. Also, I'm super anxious and upset right now and I really don't want this job and resent you already because I'm giving you the power to judge me and I don't like being judged for hating Narcan trainings and Active Shooter Drills.

EXPERIENCE

Executive Assistant/ Admissions Coordinator, New Dawn Wellness — 2013-2016 Duties

- Waiting on a bunch of people who had less education than I did but made a lot more money.
- Waking up every day, wondering if this was the day I get stabbed.
- Project management including developing and executing office procedures that nobody follows.
- Spitefully shredding things my coworkers needed.
- Getting coffee for people who can damn well get up and get it themselves.
- Crying in the bathroom for existential and personal reasons.

Some More Fucked Up Nurse Shit of 2013

- Staring in disbelief while my boss broke the law
- Saying "wait, what?" when she asked me to help he break the law.
- Cataloging the body bags she kept in the back closet as if the coroner didn't exist.
- Doing inventory and tearing my hair out because we're a small nurses office we don't need a full anesthesia kit.
- Finding dirty speculums accumulating in the drawer, including one with gum stuck to it. Fuck, I hope it was gum.

Patient Access Representative II, Large Rural Hospital - 2011-2013

- Making excuses for the manager's kid.
- Member Patient Satisfaction Committee 2013
- Doing all the overhead pages because I had the best voice.
- Staring in horror when patients hand me sandwich bags with shit in them.
- Not laughing at the ER patient with something stuck up his butt.

Email Ghost, Business Associates of America – 2010-2011

- Sitting at a dead lady's desk.
- Mild ghost busting.
- Deliberately packing boxes wrong so they didn't ask me to do it again.
- Riding book carts down the morgue ramp.
- Hiding my education because it made my boss feel threatened.

EDUCATION

- Over $35,000.00 in student Loans. HIRE ME!

LIKE AN UNPAID HOOKER, SO BEGINS MY LIFE WITH AN MA IN CREATIVE WRITING

"You'll still edit my book for free, right?" My friend's brother, Ben, texted me after he sent me a long and pedantic word document that was either his self-help memoir or Entourage Fan Fiction.

"No," I replied. "You're going to need grammar, spelling, formatting, and a few other things. I can do 75 cents a page." It was a 400page unformatted monstrosity in which he had spelled his own name wrong. Twice.

"Lol that's not what you said before."

"You didn't send it to me until now. Back then I could afford to do it for free. Now I can't. Most other freelance editors are going to charge you $2 or $3 a page."

"But we're friends."

And so continued my foray into freelance editing and copywriting.

I graduated with my Masters of Arts in Creative writing in 2010. I had mixed feelings about graduate school because my reasons for doing it weren't entirely pure. Sure, I wanted to become a better writer, but I basically should have been sitting in orientation with a t-shirt that said STILL JUST HERE FOR THE INSURANCE AND MAYBE JOB SECURITY AND SOME FRIENDS.

As the economy went tits up, I got laid off from Feel Better Pharmacy. We took the layoff as a sign and moved from the suburban Pennsylvania town where I had gone to graduate school to a small town on the New York-Canada border so my husband could go to college. We lived in a 500 square ft. two-room cabin with a roof and floor that leaked. Our landlord, a well-groomed banker type, warned us there weren't a lot of jobs available unless I wanted to be a barista.

I mean, I had the degree for it.

With my shiny new Creative Writing degree, I surprisingly found a job as a temp copywriter for a company that planned and hosted major corporate training events back in the day before they just tortured you with webinars. The company was called Business Associates of America and after two weeks without any assignments and no computer access, they put me in the warehouse to "help out" with the shipping department until they got my computer access and assignments sorted out. I spent most days lugging incredibly heavy boxes full of management textbooks around to be scanned and packed, and being spoken to about how dirty my desk area was.

The woman who I was replacing, Victoria, had died at her desk six months before they hired me and they hadn't cleaned out her cubicle yet. They wouldn't let me clean the desk since it still had almost all of Victoria's belongings; notes, planners, and assignments for the last two and a half decades along with pictures of children and grandchildren. A half-eaten jar of Nutella in the bottom drawer had turned into an ant farm and the floor was littered with gummy worms, pencil shavings, and hole punch circles. I tried to box some stuff up so I could have a small workspace and got an angry call from my boss, Diane, from across the hall to "leave everything alone and get back to work."

Colleen, one of the senior copywriters, had been Victoria's best friend so she couldn't come over to my cubicle without a deep breath and a tissue clenched in her fist. Victoria's sweater was still draped over the back of the chair, smelling like Pert Plus and Lily of the Valley.

The creep factor was boosted by the fact that the building had been a tuberculosis sanitarium back in the 1800s, and our basement office had been the morgue. Everybody tried to say it wasn't, but it was. There were random ramps and an elevator that went to a concrete and stone dock that we didn't use, and had a totally menacing Memento Mori type angel perched in the brickwork above it, leering accusingly into the parking lot which had formerly been a cemetery as evidenced by the broken and jagged tombstones poking out from the shrubs around it. The best part was the drains in the floor that were obviously totally not for blood or embalming, or at least that's what Diane said.

I was given an old IBM laptop that was heavier than a car battery to use for emails while I was across the property in the warehouse. Most days, my emails consisted of priority projects from Diane and Colleen that I had no way to work on because I had no access to anything, probably made worse because I hadn't been assigned my own email address and was still using Victoria's.

For outside vendors and people at the Manhattan office who didn't know the situation, it was awkward explaining that no, I'm not the dead lady, I'm just *temping* for her. It was even more awkward explaining to people who knew that Victoria was dead that my emails weren't haunted digital missives from the great beyond. The fact that they hired a temp should have clued me in that things were going to get weird. Did they think she was coming back?

I know the office is an old-timey morgue, but was there a plan I wasn't aware of?

* * *

After my first full month there, the charm of being an email ghost who climbed in and out of book carts and sometimes rode those book carts down the old morgue ramp wore off hard. I came in one day and found that my/Victoria's desk had been completely cleaned and moved and there was someone sitting at it.

"Megan, this is Jeannine. She's our new copywriter. Jennine, this is Megan. She's one of our warehouse helpers," Dianne introduced me to my replacement.

I opened my mouth and saw one of my coworkers make a chopping motion so I smiled and could feel my face burn. It got worse.

"Jeannine just got her associates from Florida Tech Online. She's going to be working from home Tuesday through Friday, and she'll be in the office on Mondays," Diane smiled and gave Jennine's shoulder a squeeze before going in her office and shutting the door.

My coworkers, Sharon and Paul stood there with embarrassed looks on their faces.

I later found out that Jeannine was Diane's half-sister.

For the next six months, Jeannine was late on her assignments, bad at editing, and her official office signature included this gem, complete with hot-pink comic sans:

Jeannine Fiacciacola
Coppy Editor
Copy Righter
Business Ass. of America
Class of 2010
Florida Tech Online
Associate's Degree in Liberal Arts
Mom of Jared!
3/04/2009 *Luv you baby boy*

Git 'R Done! ~ Larry the Cable Guy

Someone in the corporate HR office in Manhattan got an email with Jeannine's signature on it and we all ended up getting a very shrill and angry lecture from Diane the next day about our email signatures not being professional enough. Jeannine wasn't in the office that day.

Diane furtively called me into her office and asked me to help take some of Jeannine's workload, breaking ground for me to professionally and quietly do the work other, dumber people got credit for as well as my own.

This wasn't the first time I had been asked to edit or write content for one of my employers after they passed me over for the task the first time, when I worked at Moretto's Resort, the kitchen manager would give me the weekly menu to edit after the CEO's secretary had written "FIRST CUM FIRST SERVE" on the Memorial Day barbecue menus, but this was the first time I had a degree specializing in it.

People always seemed to really want my help editing

and writing stuff, but they didn't want to pay me for it. At Blue Line Medical Center, my boss would send me down to HR to help them write up the Christmas bulletin, or to the PR office to edit a press release.

"Why don't you just hire me to do this?" I asked the HR officer bluntly after a day of editing bulletins. She sighed.

"Sharon's been in the position since the 70s. We can't fire her."

I learned that the writing world, whether it be academia, the private sector, or online writing groups were always full of dysfunction, but writers aren't wholly functional people, are we? I deliberately took jobs that would allow me to write during my downtime, but of course my writing got me in trouble.

I kept journals in my purse for plot and story ideas along and writing exercises. At Blue Line Medical Center we weren't allowed to be seen on our phones or reading books, but writing looked like work so this worked for me until my boss asked me why I was writing stuff down all the time.

"I'm writing a book," I said. She gave me a quizzical look.

"Like, about the hospital?" Not yet, but give it time.

"No. It's about robots and like, wizards and there's like, a royal family," I said, thinking that honesty was a good thing. I was halfway through outlining a fantasy steampunk post-apocalyptic novel because it was 2012 and that's what you did back then. She gave me an even more confused look. Nicki and I weren't really close. She was an okay boss, but she had a queen of the trailer park vibe that made it hard for me to want to listen to her along with the fact that both her kids were in prison, which kind of made me question her leadership abilities.

"Why are you writing a book?"

"Why not?" I asked. She rolled her eyes at me and shrugged, the universal symbol for I'm done with this crazy asshole.

"Well, I'm going to need you to stop doing that because the ladies in the office think you're watching them and taking notes."

It's tough out there for writers, especially since having a degree for it is pretty worthless. Every copywriting job I've ever applied for just basically asked for one thing: photoshop skills. After paying for this degree, you're going to make me pay for my own software too? Fuck no. And the worst part is you end up working for people who have the literary skills of a 4Channer. Being a writer or even a copywriter can be a horrible way to make a living and you sometimes deal with horrible people, or you have to pretend to be a ghost.

I WORKED ALL DAY, WHAT DID YOU DO?

During my childhood, I frequently heard adults around me use the phrase "I *worked* all day. What did *you* do?"

This inquiry was usually directed at anybody who had a job that didn't involve the potential degradation of their physical and emotional states for a 25-year span until they got early retirement from a slipped disc. "I worked all day" is the war cry of Rural Elitism.

Various forms of it would mutate: "Um, I *work* all day" or "*Excuse me*, but I actually *work*" would pop up in conversation when people were tired, frustrated, angry, or talking about someone who just had their kitchen redone. I don't want to portray the adults of my childhood as assholes; a majority of them were far from it. They were all stressed and beat up by a system that wasn't working for them, they just weren't good at expressing that frustration. The idea of working and contributing to anything, a household, the community, loomed heavily in my mind so I internalized it and started feeling guilty at a very young age that I didn't have a job.

It was the 1990s, not the 1890s and child labor laws

aren't just guidelines so it's not like I could just go work at the factory and was choosing not to. For a span of time as a kid, (a time frame I blame on reading too much historical fiction and frequently hearing *I worked all day, what did you do?*) I actually thought I was going to leave school at 13 and get an apprenticeship. My husband, Sean, did exactly that but that's a different can of creepy religious home-schooled worms. Also, we didn't have cable, internet, or 911 on my street until I was about eleven or twelve. There were no sidewalks, and our address was Rural Delivery Route 1 until 1996 or so it's not like we had paper boys. Ten-year-olds didn't contribute to the booming economy.

I was never afraid of hard work, or even disturbing work, it was the *expectation* of work that scared me. My father was a butcher and while he worked for a popular chain grocery store by day, we ran and operated a small slaughterhouse/butcher business at home.

Some of my earliest memories at 7 years old have me outside with my sister and a few of the local teen boys my parents hired for help with hunting season. My sister and I were skinning and salting deer hides along with the boys or using a bow-saw to remove the deer's front legs. It didn't occur to me that this was work. It also didn't occur to me that it was gross. It also didn't occur to me that I was too young to be handling a bow-saw.

Everybody was just outside and I wanted to be outside, too. Especially when we'd get into fits of silliness and start hitting each other with the freshly severed forelegs, that was always fun. If it was a warm day the tendons would stay nice and loose and if you got a good grip on the stump (the good grip was crucial because the skin and sinew would slide around and the bone would poke out and mess up your aim) you could wind up and whack someone really good with the hooves. Occasionally we'd go in after a long day, wind-swept and covered in bruises like we'd gotten caught in a stampede at the North Pole.

Good times.

As I got older and spent more time with kids at school, I realized that it's not necessarily normal for a 7-year-old to know how to bone and joint an animal carcass but it wasn't 100% unusual in our town. In fact, my parents were slightly bougie about it because we had actual sterilized work areas and machinery to butcher the meat; they didn't just butcher it on the kitchen table like some of my friends' parents did.

My rural elitism was showing early on when at a sleep-over my friend's grandfather hauled a deer carcass onto the dining room table and started gleefully hacking it apart in front of a bunch of screaming ten-year-olds. I stood haughtily in the corner, arms folded, surveying the carnage and thinking *"that's not even how you separate the shoulder joint. You're going to lose so much meat doing that. This guy's got a shitty work ethic."*

It toughened me up a lot as a kid, which is probably why I hate Boy Meets World and Full House.

I WAS GUTTING ANIMALS AT YOUR AGE, YOU LITTLE PUSSIES. STOP BEING WORRIED ABOUT YOUR READING GLASSES. IF YOU NEED A SPINE I WILL GIVE YOU ONE FROM THE PILE BEHIND OUR BARN.

Working with my parents during hunting season laid the foundation for my customer service skills, which is to say they started out as abrasive and kind of stayed that way. If I wasn't skinning and salting hides or sawing off Bambi's legs, I was filling out the order forms for the hunters and doing intake. When I was nine we had a particularly busy hunting season, which always fell right between Thanksgiving and Christmas.

My father wasn't home from work yet and my mom had run out to the grocery store when a truck pulled up and two guys in work pants and orange jackets so bright it almost had a sound, started unloading a deer from their truck bed. I grabbed the clipboard, an old wooden mess covered in dark blotches of blood with a pen taped to a string on the back, and went outside. I had stepped into my Dad's swampers, the top of the boots almost coming up to my hips, and clomped down the porch steps.

It must have been a strange sight; I was growing out a mushroom cut and had thrown on my Mom's bedazzled acid wash denim jacket so I probably looked like if one of the Lollipop Guild had decided to go full on Ted Kaczynski, or maybe if an Oompa Loompa had joined a union and was conducting a door-to-door survey. The hunters grinned at me because, let's face it, I looked stupid yet earnestly determined and adults love that shit.

"Fill this out and you can hang the carcass here," I handed the one guy the clipboard and pointed to the meat hooks hanging from the A-Frame that used to be our swing set. Still grinning, the guy handed me back the clipboard. I checked his hunting tag to make sure it was a legal kill and he grinned even wider.

"Can I pay ahead?" He reached for his wallet.

"Small bills only, I don't have change," I said. Both of them were looking at each other with extreme amusement at the homeless leprechaun bossing them around. The guy reached for his wallet and handed me a twenty.

"It's forty dollars," I said. His eyes sparkled and he was thoroughly enjoying haggling with a kid.

"Last year your dad did it for twenty."

"No, he didn't," I said. We didn't haggle and we didn't make special arrangements. Our rate was a flat $40 no matter what.

"He did though," the hunters' companion snorted and got back in the truck.

"No, he didn't."

Still entertained and not annoyed in any way, the guy grinned again. "Well Boss Lady, if that's how it is, I'll just pay when I pick it up." He winked at me and got in the truck.

It turns out my dad did have a special arrangement with this guy where he just quartered the deer and gave him the rest as soup bones, charging him half price. Being nine and not knowing the inner workings of upper management, I stubbornly stuck to my guns, which entertained the gentleman to no end. When he came to pick up his order, he asked my parents where the CEO was and told them the story of how I basically brow-beat him until he left. They all had a good laugh and he paid and picked up his order. He came down past where I was skinning and stopped.

"Hey, Boss Lady!" I turned around, a boning knife in my little pink-mittened hand. He tucked a twenty in it.

"You're a hard nut to crack. Merry Christmas, kid." He left, still chuckling to himself.

Getting off work and watching Stephanie Tanner struggle with a lemonade stand had me rolling my 8-year-old eyes. I looked down on her because her biggest life struggles being bad catchphrase and getting reading glasses were the embodiment of Rural Elitism: I believe my struggle has made me a better person and your lack of struggle has made you a weaker person and I resent you because until I saw how you lived, I didn't realize I wasn't middle class. My struggle *has* to be morally superior because if it isn't, *what am I doing it for?*

It is the essential core of a combination of working-class martyrdom and ignorant superiority comprised of a mindset that encompasses the following tenants:

• Real work breaks you down physically and mentally.

• All authority is absolute, be it family or management.

• Higher education is for the weak and lazy.

• Artists and creative people are mentally ill and selfish.

• People on welfare are lazy assholes unless you need it and then only you deserve it.

I could just keep making a miserable bullet list of all the crazy shit I've heard over the years but basically what I got from rural elitism is the belief that I am not worth anything unless I'm physically breaking myself down for as little money as possible and that being happy is a goal for unrealistic assholes.

This work ethic followed me through many different careers and I still grapple with the idea that I don't matter because I'm not hurling myself against the cogs of capitalism for $9.50 an hour to the detriment of my physical and mental health.

In graduate school, I worked at a furniture warehouse, dusting end tables for $7.50 an hour. I called out one day because I was drastically behind with my school work and then spent that day in a panic that I would be fired from a minimum wage job where most staff members skimmed from the register and showed up drunk.

Rural elitism established an insurmountable authority in my life where every time I sought out a creative job or paying project, I thought there was some kind of judgment or punishment waiting in the wings. I always aimed for shitty menial jobs like scrubbing toilets and stocking shelves because I didn't think I was smart enough or worth anything else—if I made a mistake or even thought I had made one, I would tailspin in an endless panic.

Once I was in college around a lot of privileged white kids I felt the need to suffer even more and started working 30-hour weeks, sometimes 3 separate part-time jobs, sometimes one full-time job. I'd go to class form 9-3 and then work 3:30 to 10 and 12 hours on Saturday.

I was still broke when I graduated undergrad with a lower-than-it-should-have-been GPA.

After living, working, and going to college in mostly rural conservative bubbles since 2005, I have had my education and subsequent challenging of rural elitism be called conversion therapy for liberals.

I've frequently been asked to explain myself to someone with a Confederate Flag tattoo exactly *why* I "wasted all that money on college." The last time I was asked this question it was from a distant relative who had just spent $20,000 on a new tractor so he could enter the state tractor pull competition. For twenty minutes he had been waxing philosophic on the merits of being a professional "puller" and how if he won the state championship, he'd have $5,000 in prize money to fix his truck. The concept of a false economy didn't even exist to this earnest young man who did not see the giant financial problem in having a high monthly payment on a piece of equipment he was going to abuse until it had no equity left for the potential of *maybe* winning $5,000 to fix his truck. The inexplicable part of this was that he had actually managed to make me feel bad about myself.

Rural elitism dictates that you either make insanely stupid purchases or you never spend money on anything, ever. While my husband was in college and I was working for Business Associates of America, we had several months of high-powered clients who needed coddling and I ended up with 30 hours of overtime on one paycheck.

We had a Whirlpool Washer and Dryer that were given to us by somebody's relocating aunt or uncle. The set was 25 years old and barely worked. The washer didn't drain most of the time and finally caused a flood in our small apartment. The belt in the dryer had melted to the drum and had set our comforter on fire. Being continually broke students, we reveled in my OT windfall and marched to Sears to buy a gleaming new washer and dryer set with a warranty. The level of shit we got from our relatives for spending money on something practical that we needed was the epitome of rural elitism.

"You spent money on that? Take it back! Demand a refund!" said my mother-in-law, as if we'd been tricked into buying it and didn't research our purchase and pick it out deliberately.

"What were you *thinking*?" hissed one of our siblings. "That's so irresponsible of you!"

"I can't believe you didn't just fix it! Those were great machines! $20 and a trip to the dump would have had you back in business!" One of our relatives was a proponent of just going to the dump and rummaging until he found the piece he needed, or a piece that looked kind of like the piece he needed which he would then hit with a hammer until it worked. His dishwasher had a pair of vice-grips holding a lawn mower battery and a clump of wires together and you had to turn it on with insulated gloves. He was risking electrocution every time he wanted to do dishes and 90% of the time they came out just as dirty as they went in, but he didn't spend any money fixing it, which obviously meant he was going straight to the front of the line in Heaven. His washer and dryer had started bigger fires than ours did, and he had to manually drain his washer but hey, he wasn't a sucker like we were.

How to create financial security and execute smart spending isn't something that's taught to a lot of rural children, as evidenced by our washer and dryer and the limp-it-until-it-dies mentality. Fixing what you have is what hard workers do, even if it eventually becomes a bad investment: from trying to DIY the repairs to having a repairman come to fix it repeatedly, you're showing moral superiority by struggling. There's no martyrdom spending $350 in trying to fix your washing machine if a brand new one costs $243, that just means you're dumb. Sean and I created a new phrase to combat the overreaction to buying our washer and dryer: *I'm too poor to buy cheap shit.* That argument worked and we got a lot of "well, you're right" chuckles. But it didn't translate into college or spending money on education to have better job prospects.

While I got two degrees that are basically a $50,000 I shrug when someone asks "what are you going to do with that?" Sean actually got a useful degree and, hold on to your asses, *got a job in his field right out of college.* I know, right? Who the fuck does he think he is? And what's worse is that he's making the world a better place because he's a federal scientist who specializes in water quality and safety while I'm over here thinking my thoughts are important enough for people to buy.

The flip side of money confusion is my aforementioned puller buddy and machine hoarder who has five trucks, two snowmobiles (sleds, he called them) three four-wheelers (quads) and what he said was a classic car chassis but looked like '99 Chevy. He and his girlfriend were constantly getting their power shut off and his girlfriend desperately tried to hawk MLM products like Lularoe and Mary Kay to make up for all the dumb financial choices they made. But they were smug, proud of the fact, and even though I had an education, I was still in debt like the rest of them.

"I'll bet you think you're better than me!" is a phrase I have heard a lot at barbeques I no longer go to.

"Look at Joe College over here! The Marines not good enough for you, college boy?" people would jokingly ask my husband as if his spine and hip weren't permanently damaged at the age of 19. As if he didn't earn the GI bill he used.

In my nuclear family, I'm the only one who finished college. While both my parents started but didn't finish college, they each held down small businesses and 30 year careers and were voracious readers. I grew up in a house where no topic was off limits if I was reading. My sister ran a local business for over a decade and I think she only called out sick twice in ten years while I'm over here job hopping because I don't like how the lady in the cubicle next to me smells. One time I called in sick because I had the hiccups and didn't feel like getting dressed. True story. When I was a kid, I overheard my Godmother tell my mom that she broke a tooth at the beginning of a shift and just super glued it back together and kept pushing on because dentists were expensive and, shrug, it's not like it hurt.

Rural elitism is a creature on the verge of a major evolutionary event with one foot on a banana peel and the other in the grave and a third vestigial foot just kind of dangling there twitching. Some people, like my parents, know that as the world changes your children will reap opportunities that weren't available to you at that age. Other people just lose their shit and think "oh fuck my kid's going to be smarter than me" and then take it to a toxic place. For me, my adult life has been an exhausting tilt of waiting for the cultural comet to wipe out this way of life while trying to guess where I'm being too smart and what kind of too smart I'm being. Am I being intimidatingly too smart? Am I being condescending and too smart? Am I not being smart enough?

Usually, it ends up not mattering anyway because even after the not really that fancy schooling, rural elitism follows me still, sitting at my elbow as I write this, pointing out that nobody cares what I have to say and that I'm not better than anybody. It's a mentality that fosters a locked in class system, it tells you that education is for rich people who don't work hard. Rural elitism, in its purest and most toxic form, is the boiled down essence of Isaac Asimov's "My ignorance is just as good as your knowledge."

HR OWES MY BOOBS AN APOLOGY

"Okay, but what about Megan!?" I heard an angry shout from the closed-door nurse manager's office. I put my head on my desk in annoyance. I could still hear loud voices that sounded like a livestream YouTube debate. I knew where this was going, or more what this would be about—my tits.

Look, I think I have the sex appeal of a wet badger who just put on her pajamas and wants to eat her Lime Green Jell-O in peace, but I'm also aware I'm a woman with DDs in a world where people fucking suck, so I'm incredibly cautious when it comes to how low cut my shirts are. My work attire became a rotation of different Old Navy polos, usually men's and usually three sizes too big, zip up fleeces, librarian cardigans, and khakis. And yet, I periodically got spoken to about my tits by people who seemed really offended that I wasn't more apologetic about them, especially since I was wearing the scrubs or uniforms *they* issued, one of which had a V neck that came down to my ribcage. After starting at New Dawn Wellness, a halfway house for homeless men, I held my breath and waited. I knew what was coming when Nancy came out of the office, pinching the bridge of her nose.

The door opened and I heard Nancy ask, "Megan, can you come in here a minute?"

"Why?" I was going to make her work for it. Nancy shifted nervously.

"We've had a complaint that you're dressed inappropriately."

"Is it because I'm dressed like a manager at Best Buy?" I asked, lowering my voice conspiratorially. Nancy gave me a flat stare and chewed on the inside of her cheek.

I didn't want to give her the opportunity to gain steam. Nancy's Dress Test included putting your arms out in front of you so she could gauge where your boobs were or something. I had on a polo shirt that was buttoned to the collar and nobody in HR should ever be telling anybody "put your arms out and face the wall."

"Megan," she huffed. "don't make this difficult."

"I'm dressed like a nun on vacation. This is bullshit."

"Megan, it's not bullshit, it's just that...the problem..." she trailed off. "We might need to send you home to change."

"The problem is the size of my breasts, not the cut of my shirt. You had a problem with the size of my breasts even though last time Kayla wore pants so tight you could see her labia. Yet, Kayla still works here and I'm the one being sent home to change. So since this is the second time you've had to talk to me about my tits I'm assuming this place is either going to pay for my breast reduction, buy me a boob shrinking raygun,"

She stared at me with wide, owl eyes. Saying nothing.

"Or," I said, "I'm assuming you'll just settle for a sexual harassment suit?"

"Harassment?" she said, shrilly.

"Well, yeah. So far it's only harassment, but if you touch me, and I'm not sure what you're doing with this arms to your side and face the wall shit, but it sounds like you're going to touch me, that's assault. And that costs at least double what I charge at the truck stop."

"Costs....double...," she muttered to herself. After a minute of staring at me in abject horror, she started giggling. She sat down with an explosive cackle that turned into braying laughter for almost a full solid minute.

"Jesus Christ," she sniffled when she was done. "You can go back to work. I'm sorry for bothering you."

"I'm serious," I said, holding the door open for her. She stopped giggling and looked at me.

"Okay. It won't happen again."

It happened four more times before I quit six months later.

THE 7 COWORKERS YOU'LL HATE —
PLUS KEVIN

The average American holds down 11.7 different jobs in their lifetime from 18 years old to retirement. I thought I made that statistic up but when I bothered to do research—I was pretty damn close to being accurate. That's a lot of job switching.

When we think of why people leave their jobs we think it's for a positive reason: new job with more money and better benefits. We give too much power to the myth of upward mobility and the happy American office. I'm here to say that painting the walls neo-hippie friendly colors and buying us pizza on Fridays doesn't fucking work. Pizza and the color-wheel won't cure the sickness of being around your coworkers.

You don't need a PhD in sociology to know that people leave their jobs because they hate their coworkers. If you think I'm lying, peruse social media at 5:30pm on a Friday and see how much thinly veiled bullying and passive aggression you can stomach.

And all the wine jokes.

We get it, Karen, you're an alcoholic.

Every time I would quit a job or requested a transfer, I was usually close to committing involuntary man-slaughter or what I'd call "righteous murder." Or even a felony worse than murder—sending out passive aggressive e-mails.

There are definitely better jobs but there are no better co-workers. I ended up working with essentially the same group of people at every workplace.

I believe that I'm in a Truman-Show type experiment, being studied by scientists who have created these people (they could be reptilians but that is for another book) to psychologically test my homicidal rages. Because these same seven coworkers are at every shitty job I've had.

Don't tell Alex Jones, but I think I'm onto a clone conspiracy.

Management Material Martha

Early forties, has been working for the company since she was 22, Martha is still really pissed that she didn't get promoted to manager even though she knows *way* more than the current manager. She's always storming in to the office or storming out of the office, yelling at her kids, or her husband loudly on her cell phone, which is still a flip phone. She has a Kate Gosselin haircut.

Everything is an inconvenience and people are obviously out to get her: clients, the company, coworkers, our boss, her husband, and especially her mother-in-law.

Takes 8 smoke breaks a day. Has one purse, two tote bags and one lunch box, can never find her lighter.

Is always on a diet until someone makes her mad.

These Colors Don't Run Carl

Super nice until you tell him no, Carl is usually found in management. He and *Management Material Martha* get along well if Martha isn't working for him. He is the only person who does any real work (he actually likes the job) and calls you lazy when you ask for a day off and gets mad at women for going on maternity leave. Very grossed out by periods. Carl doesn't like his kids. He likes to listen to Rush Limbaugh but thinks Alex Jones goes too far. You can tell you're nearing Carl's territory because he has a lot of Americana around his desk, including and not limited to a Don't Tread on Me Flag and if he is nearing retirement a Confederate flag even though this is New York.

Totally Not A Pyramid Scheme Brianna

Don't buy anything from Brianna. Just don't do it. Say no when she tries to sell you the skin firming wraps which are really just paper towels soaked in moisturizer, diet green tea powder, the diet coffee powder, the diet shake powder, the diet pills, and the infuser oils that smell like a koala took a shit in your house. Brianna doesn't have a high school diploma but she's an expert in dermatology, dietary nutrition, and curing asthma with essential oils. Doesn't believe in evolution. Brianna is on a diet.

What is Linux, Lynda

Lynda is Martha's biggest competition; like two angry alpha bitch tigers fighting over a zebra carcass, Martha and Lynda fight about everything. Nothing is off limits: kids, grandkids, spouses. It's all personal. Lynda is in her late fifties and has been working for the company longer than Donna and wants you to know it. She shares traits with *These Colors Don't Run Carl* in that she is also the only person who does actual work and doesn't complain about it. Lynda thinks webinars are on par with getting chlamydia, and has been known to wipe out the shared drive with a virus from a chain email about a little girl with cancer who was healed by Christ's love. She likes to use all caps in emails, swears she doesn't know how to import data so she doesn't have to do end of month reports but plays candy crush on her brand new iPhone during lunch break and afterwork gets into Facebook fights with randos. She is on a diet.

My Mom Works Here Todd

Todd's mom got him this job and because everybody is afraid of Todd's mom, nobody reports him for being a dumbfuck. Todd is always late, smells like weed, and usually dresses like somebody meeting their parole office. Yet, *These Colors Don't Run Carl* thinks Todd is management material and has a great head on his shoulders. Todd calls out a lot at the last minute usually because he's hungover or drunk, asks to leave early all the time, and generally makes a lot of mistakes. He quotes The Simpsons a lot. Clients and customers don't like Todd because Todd is dumb. Martha and Lynda love Todd and bring him cupcakes because he is too skinny. Todd is in his early thirties, balding, and not a fan of immigrants even though he's never met one. He looks at porn on his phone during work. He's currently trying to fuck Brianna.

Karen's Eating Clean For Her Wedding

If it feels like Karen's engagement and wedding planning have been sucking out parts of your soul, it's because it has. Karen is in her mid-twenties and just graduated with her Associate's degree. Her boyfriend only proposed last month but it feels like it was twenty years ago. Any projects she was working on prior to her engagement no longer matter and she will stare at Pinterest for about 80% of the day. Brianna is selling Karen diet pills.

Brotrapeneuer Tony

Tony's is just working here until his business takes off. It's never clear what his business is, but it involves gym equipment, an app, nudity, &/or his uncle from Florida. Don't invest in Tony's business but it's not a bad idea to buy him some new cologne because his cubicle stinks like Drakkar Noir and beer farts.

Kevin

Every office has a Kevin, probably bearded, and probably working in IT. Sometimes Kevin works in Human Resources, or he's a security guard, or he's in your department as the decent guy who helps out. He likes *Lord of The Rings* and has a sword collection but not in a weird way. His girlfriend drops off his lunch in a HufflePuff t-shirt and they're planning a Dr. Who themed wedding that you really hope you get invited to. Kevin is a treasure and too good for this world. Always be nice to Kevin.

I WAS GOING TO BUY A HOUSE, BUT I
BOUGHT THIS AVOCADO INSTEAD

"You're not special!" Mrs. Stone, my third-grade teacher screamed in the face of a hunched over a crying little boy holding a note.

It was 1992 and I was seven. Mrs. Stone was famous among all the kids of my elementary school, including the ones who never had her, for her lectures about responsibility, for screaming and yelling, throwing things and punching the desks and walls. She even put her fist through the overhead projector. I was there for the projector punching. There was a fabled rumor the older kids would tell us that she actually punched a kid in the face once. I don't doubt that story.

The little boy in question (I feel like his name was Tommy) had handed her a note stapled to his blank worksheet. In our eight-year-old world, there was no shame worse than a blank worksheet. We were supposed to line up every morning and hand in our homework (a packet of worksheets), and if you didn't have your homework, you got screamed at, lost recess for a week, and got snide remarks made about you to the rest of the class until the next unlucky soul forgot *their* worksheets and the cycle began anew. Parents, including mine, had made some complaints about Mrs. Stone and that maybe it was time for her to retire, but the administration sided with her when she took away recess for the entire week because a kid sneezed and didn't say "excuse me."

Mrs. Stone read the note and examined the blank sheet, her face getting blotchy and red. "Why should you get special treatment?" She pounded the desk with her fist to punctuate each word. "A note from your mother isn't going to get you out of not doing your homework." she snarled, her glasses inches from his tear-stained face.

"But my grandpa died last night," he eked out between sobs.

Then he puked on her desk.

We were all sent down early to gym, and the little boy whose grandpa died was sent to the school nurse to calm down. I can imagine how *that* phone call went, having to tell the kid's parents that his teacher screamed at him because his grandpa died.

When we got back to class we had a classroom monitor give us more worksheets to do while Mrs. Stone cleaned barf off her desk and muttered angrily at us under her breath. The little boy whose grandpa passed away was out for the rest of the week. His parents moved to a different school district shortly after; I don't know if that's related but I feel like it is.

From a very early age I was frequently told I wasn't special or more deserving or more important than someone else, which is why the special snowflake millennial label confuses me. Even the label "millennial" confuses me because I was born in 1985 and after multiple internet searches, I could be a Millennial, a Xennnial, Late Term Gen-Xer, The Real Gen Z, or a few other things that also sound like complicated sex toys.

The idea that my generation was coddled and told what special individuals we were by our parents and teachers is a myth that I find surprisingly annoying. The only time I was told I was special or more deserving than others was when my whiteness was taken into account, and then my special-ness was a given, which makes the term "special snowflake" even potentially shittier than it already is. It took me an embarrassingly long time to let go of that shitty idea.

Over the years I worked for managers and bosses who screamed and came unglued over small inconveniences and I was always able to deal with them, so I know that Mrs. Stone is somewhere in hell, boiling in a kettle of cat piss, smiling and happy because she knows she taught me to withstand shitty authority figures.

Far from being called special, I was threatened with the adult world of ham-faced angry bosses before I was ten. Mrs. Stone was fond of responding to every wrong answer with "do you think you'd keep your job if you answered your boss like that?"

The third grade was peppered with an intense amount of threats about the bleakness of adulthood.

If Mrs. Stone was still alive she would nod approvingly at all the recent headlines and clickbait about the lazy, enti-tled, special snowflake millennial who spends thousands of dollars on avocados and raw water instead of saving for retirement. According to mainstream and alternative media, we're all ungrateful beta cucks who live with our parents and refuse to get jobs, so we can follow our passions, and desperately want meaning in our work while trying to kill off chain restaurants.

I'm not sure how we're all lazy assholes who don't work because by 2020 Millennials will make up about 75% of the US workforce. We already make up 75% of the US military, and, hold onto your butts: 57% of veterans from the Global War on Terror are lazy, entitled, crybaby snowflake millennials who don't understand hard work, many of whom were in active combat before the age of 20.

One trip to Google confirms that my generation is getting a lot of negative attention for just trying to exist in this world when wages are stagnant and 63% of us have more than $10,000 in student debt. To understand a millennial's position in the economy, we need to dispel some labels and myths.

The Special Snowflake Millennial

The myth that millennials were raised by codling helicopter parents and praised relentlessly by crunchy granola teachers telling us we were such special individuals is easily dispelled, as evidenced by my experience in Mrs. Stone's 3rd-grade classroom. I have never been told by a parent, teacher, babysitter, coach, advisor, counselor, professor or any other adult in my life that I was special. Adults frequently went out of their way to tell me the opposite. I never got a participation trophy, and I was never called a snowflake nor was I told that I was a precious and important individual. I've only ever been called a special snowflake (mostly on Twitter with people with Anime avatars) as an insult.

"Snowflake" has been co-opted by the alt-right and angry boomers on Facebook to be an insult blanket term to attack the mentally ill, the traumatized, and people who actually like to be their authentic selves.

The earliest known usage of the term goes back to the 1860s and the beginning of the Civil War where "snowflake" or "snowball" was someone who opposed the abolition of slavery, claiming white superiority. So the first snowflakes were angry privileged dudes who didn't want to lose their safe spaces...I mean Plantations.

In 1996 Chuck Palahniuk graced us with Fight Club and the notion of the "special snowflake" got picked-up in pop culture. I've noticed it's especially a favorite of conservatives and baby boomers, which is weird because it's an anti-capitalist counter-culture phrase coined by a mentally ill man and a gay author. If my Facebook feed is accurate, nobody hates anti-capitalists, counter-culture thought, gays, or the mentally-ill more than baby-boomers and conservatives.

By the time the idea of the special snowflake hit pop-culture I was already past those tender years of developing self-confidence. So it begs the question: if the concept never existed in a positive state and didn't even exist in its negative state until half way through our childhoods, how could we have been raised as "special individual snowflakes"?

Lazy Ass Millennials

More than one-third of working millennials have more than one job. That doesn't count the ones with cash only businesses like lawn care, child care, contracting, or some weird Etsy store filled with ugly burlap shit (Sorry Karen, but your Live, Laugh, Love signs are cringe af.) A 2016 study by Project Time Off identifies millennials as "work martyrs" or not wanting to be seen as lazy, working over-time, not taking sick or vacation days even if they're offered as a benefit. Work martyrdom also makes my generation less likely to ask for things like paid time off, health care, and sick time.

A refrain I heard while growing up was "make sure your boss knows you're irreplaceable." After being privy to a lot of private corporate communication, I can assure you, employees are seen as 100% disposable unless they've been working there since the 70's and everyone feels bad for them. Mind you, feels bad for them, not values them.

As a generation, we're also really tired of unethical working conditions, be it low pay, a bullying or sexist working environment, or a physically unsafe working envi-ronment.

Workers are being exploited and told they can't unionize or bargain collectively for basic human treatment from their employer.

Lookin' at you, Bezos and Wal-Mart.

When I worked at Feel Better Pharmacy we were told if any of us tried to unionize we would be fired, and there was a gag policy through HR that stated we couldn't discuss HR policies amongst ourselves and we were forced to use sick time to use the bathroom during work hours.

This led to a pregnant woman wetting herself during the workday.

After being faced with having to use my vacation time to take a piss at work, I resolved to stop working for compa-nies that treated me that way. Therefore, if things got unprofessional, I would quit and find something else.

It's called "caring about my mental health and safety."

It's a strange concept, I know.

Entitled Millennials

It's difficult to understand the logic behind raising an entire generation to believe that there were certain types of work that was beneath them and then get mad at them for not gleefully storming fast food joints when the economy tanks and the degree they were pressured into taking out loans for is now potentially worthless.

We are not entitled. We just want what our parents had and took advantage of: a good economy. Harvard annual tuition in 1971 was $2,600 and now, in 2018 it is estimated around $49,480. That's a 163% increase in tuition. How much have wages increased? Not enough to justify that kind of tuition hike.

If I'm paying that much to re-read Much Ado About Nothing for the 4th time since my Junior Year in public high school, you can bet your ass I'll have expectations and feel entitled. I better get something out of it, preferably a job with livable wages. Don't give me shit about college kids being too coddled. If I'm paying that much money per semester, get me a butler to read to me. Coddle me, draw me a bath. If tuition is going to cost me up to $100,000 before I even have the capacity to bring in a salary, college better have perks like Wagyu beef and gold flake chocolate soufflé in the cafeteria and all the safe spaces I want because I can check books out of the library for free.

If millennials seem a little cranky to you, please rest assured it's because our Kombucha scoby didn't bloom and not because we could potentially be criminally punished for our debt and then hobbled without a way to pay it back. Most of us are also still really pissed off about having to wait so long for a Veronica Mars comeback and not the fact that currently 22 states in the US will revoke your professional license for unpaid or defaulted student debt, with the most frequent licenses revoked being teaching and nursing licenses, or as I like to call them "just a woman." We're going so far as a society that we're punishing people for wanting to gain experience and education to help others. And if that shit isn't enough, as of 2018, Montana, Iowa, and Oklahoma will revoke your driver's license if you've defaulted on your student loans.

If you've defaulted on your student loans, you can also lose your Social Security benefits so now my generation has to be doubly worried about saving for retirement. The bubble mortgage crisis, problematically high maternal mortality rate, and criminally low wages aside, one could see how we'd all be a little freaked out about our futures and therefore spend a lot of time taking pictures of our food to distract ourselves from the extreme likelihood of being homeless by the time we're in our sixties.

That being said, does anybody want to cosign a business loan with me so I can open an artisanal avocado toast restaurant where I serve the toast to you on a dirty garden towel?

THE TIME TRAVELER'S PENIS

Humanity is batshit. There's no way around it. And sometimes that batshittery just kind of falls in your lap — times when you're minding your own business, walking down the street and suddenly you see a rat humping a soda can. You don't know why, but the rat is going for it and the soda can is just sitting there because it's inert recycling. Anthropomorphizing the can in this scenario doesn't help us — don't look for reasons in the batshit.

Just enjoy it for the free show that it is.

You just have to take the battshittery when it comes. I thought I had a full and storied understanding of human nature from working a few jobs in retail and babysitting for a few weeks one summer when I was a teenager. I did not.

I got a job working for a popular office supply store in their copy department in the Catskills. I was on summer break between my sophomore and junior year of college and my husband was deployed to Iraq. Sounds like a real bummer, but that's when I met the time traveler.

We had a local dick toucher who hung around the store and needed the cops called on him regularly. He would wander around rubbing his dong through his sweatpants and stare at the customers. He also enjoyed using the self-service copiers to photocopy pornographic cartoons. He didn't take them with him; he left them around the store like awful greeting cards. You haven't lived until you've had an angry Hasidic mother furiously waving a color copy of a popular fairytale prince getting Eiffel Towered by a genie and a monkey in your face while she yells at you in Yiddish.

Sometimes he came in with journals filled with something that looked like math but included a lot of realistic looking sketches of testicles in the margins. He'd mutter to himself and pull his coat closed over him while he made copies and looked around furtively. A few times we caught him trying to photocopy his dick.

Besides excelling in making people uncomfortable and self-induced crotch friction, this knob polishing enthusiast was also a mixed media artist. His last great achievement was a large piece of poster board covered with thousands of pictures of penises, cut out of magazines with disturbing finesse and accuracy. He wanted it laminated.

This popular chain store was pretty clear about their policies on copying and distributing pornography: don't. But this wasn't copying pornography, it was preserving it and making it waterproof for reasons I don't want to think about.

I refused to laminate the pork sword mural, so my coworker Adam laughingly held his hand out for the poster. His face froze as the paper hit his palm. He was still smiling, as was Captain Dong. Adam's face was frozen in a weak grin but his eyes were wide with horror. As he pulled the poster across the countertop, a whiff of mushrooms and protein hit the air.

"Oh God," Adam said weakly, still smiling. "Oh, Dear

Jesus. He mixed cum in the glue." Captain Cock Rubber grinned even wider as he furiously rubbed his crotch.

I called the cops.

Adam, still horrified but unable to stop himself, ran the visual cock cacophony through the commercial laminator that we kept at 302 degrees. The baked semen smell got stronger and he smiled wider as Adam delicately moved the poster through the heat rollers. Adam had gotten himself into this and couldn't get himself out. Every time he touched the poster he'd gently wipe his hands on his shirt, like Lady Macbeth trying to rid themselves of invisible jizz particles and regicide.

The cops showed up fast and they didn't enter quietly.

Major General Boner saw them as they entered and stuck his hand under his bulky coat and *finally* grabbed something that wasn't his penis. He saw the first cop, a woman, and screamed, "FUCK YOU WHORE" and threw something heavy at her. After it hit the floor and splattered, we became aware that it was a bottle of piss, quite the latent vintage from its potency. He turned to run and got clothes-lined by another cop behind him.

He was cuffed and escorted out, providing us with a chorus of new obscenities that I had to look up on Urban Dictionary later. The cop apologized about the piss-splosion all over a rack of merchandise: an entire end-cap of Banana-gram games had gotten soaked and needed to be thrown out. I can't look at the little zip-up fruits to this day without imagining some guy rubbing his custard launcher. Before they pulled him out the double doors, he lurched violently once more against the police officer's grasp. "You don't understand!" He bellowed. "I'm from the future!"

And that's how I met my first time-traveler and why I believe in paying workers $15.00 per hour.

DRIVING ASHLEY HOME

The backseat of my Chevy was packed with plastic bags full of damp clothes that lingered like stale clove cigarettes. I didn't smoke, still don't, but Ashley did. She was small and pale and looked twelve instead of nineteen. Her hair was a faded Kool Aid blue turning green that highlighted the unhealthy undertones of her skin. She sunk back into her black Carhartt hoodie, biting at the dirty chipped nail polish on her hands, and then rubbing the spit on paint splattered jeans. I could see her as the firecracker best friend to the good girl main character in a Jennifer McMahon novel or as the adorably troubled teen who just needs love and understanding in some fraught teen tragedy show about suicide on Netflix.

But she wasn't any of those things; curled up on my passenger seat, smoking even though I asked her not to and giving me a self -conscious grimace when I asked her to roll down her window. Her teeth were a mess — Mountain Dew in the baby bottle kind of fucked up. Her dirty boots left marks on my seat, but asking for courtesy from someone like

Ashley would end in one or both of us being annoyed for the rest of the drive from Oneonta to Roscoe.

Ashley was in my Intro to Shakespeare class. Every Monday morning I'd see her slumped backwards in her chair, short and sullen, her eyes bulging with fear when the sorority girls would walk past her to their desks; tanned to orange in the middle of an Oneonta winter, with their flat-ironed hair and shrill, heat seeking laughs that sounded like they were directed at you even when they weren't. To me they were white noise, but to Ashley they were apex preda-tors. Each Monday she eyed them wearily, waiting for bullying that never came.

I was a sophomore living in the sober dorms, a building of single rooms peopled by students who either didn't want to have to grow up and face icky things like alcohol and sex, or students who didn't have the energy for that kind of life anymore. It suited me well.

After dropping out of theater school the year before, I basically should have worn a t-shirt that said I'M JUST HERE FOR THE INSURANCE PLEASE DON'T TALK TO ME. Between the summer of my freshman and sophomore year, I had been diagnosed with an aggressively painful degenerative muscle disease. Being terrified of going on Medicaid because I could think of nothing worse than being on welfare before I turned 20, I transferred schools to stay on my mother's insurance. It's safe to say I had started to give up on the narrative that college was the time in your life where the world fell into place. Ashley lived several rooms down from me. She was a freshman and lived in Roscoe, a small rural town on the way to my mom's house. We were matched up on the share-a-ride board by our bubbly resident advisor, a squat girl named Brittany who wore Winnie the Pooh t-shirts and belted Disney songs in your face mid-conversation.

The first time I dropped her off was in October on a day so blue it hurt, and she had a huge garbage bag full of clothes that she heaved unapologetically in the back of my car, next to my neat laundry bags. After a few awkward attempts at making conversation, I stopped trying to talk. She gave me a sideways glance and jabbed at my radio to find the one radio station we could get on the drive: a country station from our hometown called Thunder Country 101. It was a lot of Allen Jackson and 1990's Reba which after listening to for an hour began to feel like audible menstrual cramps. She stared out the window the entire time, giving me an uncomfortable blink when I stopped to get gas and came back with coffee for her. It sat in the center console, untouched.

When we got to Roscoe, Ashley squirmed and pulled at a cuticle and wouldn't give me her address. It was common knowledge that a lot of people in Roscoe weren't doing well financially after really bad flooding in the spring of 2005. People died in that flood, and a lot of people were displaced. I'd heard stories about families fighting with FEMA and kids getting pneumonia and almost dying from living inside damp campers and Winnebagos with no heat during the April snows.

Like most of the Catskills, it had once been a stop on the Borscht Belt trail for tourists coming out of Manhattan. The only thing saving their economy was that it was strategically placed for gas and food on Route 17 for people coming up from the city or down from Binghamton. Some economy came from Willowemoc and Beaver Kill rivers and the bored CEOs who wanted to try fly fishing.

When I was a kid there were Tipper Gore types from

Manhattan trying to boycott the area, wanting to change the names of the Beaver Kill and Fish Kill rivers to something "less violent and more animal friendly" but the problem with privilege is that you don't have look shit up; that people just let you talk and you don't have to realize that *"kill"* is the Dutch word for *"river."* It didn't occur to anybody that the town would economically suffer, but that's pretty much what living in the Catskills was like. If that doesn't encompass living at the whims of a bunch of classist assholes, nothing does.

I understood Ashley's hesitation to give me her address. It wasn't anything I hadn't seen before but I understood that she was probably embarrassed. Poverty didn't shock me, but I realize that I must have been exactly what she was afraid of. I had my own car. I had a debit card. I was just another rich kid to her.

She had me drop her off in front of a pizza place her uncle owned. I offered to help her carry her stuff in, but she wrenched the plastic bag out of my grip and almost slammed the door on my hand.

A broad faced man with a happy smile and long brown beard came bouncing out of the pizza place, a sauce splattered apron stretched over his big belly and a worm of mozzarella caught in his long beard. He scooped Ashley up and I almost saw her smile before her dirty boots touched the cracked sidewalk again. He offered me a large hand to shake and I came away dusted with flour.

"Are you one of Ashley's college friends?" He asked, looking between me and Ashley.

I saw her face, on the edge of relaxed, snap shut again into creases and her mouth screwed tight over her sharp teeth. The way he said *college*, the emphasis shaped like a punchline, made me flinch a little.

"We live in the same building," I said, playing with my keys.

Ashley stared at me like she was trying to melt me, or make me evaporate. I know that stare. Please go before you see too much. Please go before you know too much. Please go before you judge me harder.

"You're from here or Liberty?" Her uncle asked, indicating one town over with a crumpled cigarette he'd unearthed from the under his apron.

"Woodbourne," I said.

"Lotsa Jews there," he said.

I stayed silent as Ashley disappeared into the pizza place. Her uncle tried to give me cash for gas.

"I know Ashely can't pay you nothin' fer gas. Let me give you some money," he patted his pockets aimlessly. He didn't have any money on him. I knew he didn't and he knew I knew he didn't.

I was suddenly aware of every hair out of place, the small grease stain on my USMC hoodie, the rips in the knees of my jeans not being fashionable college kid rips, but trashy these are my driving home rips. I didn't want to be here, staring at the sign that said Welcome To Trout Town, USA with this man and his niece, looking at the crumbling rural decay all around me. College was supposed to make me better than this.

I should have been picking apples with a boyfriend who was double majoring in business and poetry, while our smart yet down-to-Earth friends took black and white pictures of us clustered around a bonfire with someone singing huskily into the twilight. College was where I was finally going to come into my own or at least that's what all those fucking Freddie Prinze Junior movies told me. College wasn't supposed to be a grim white knuckle through the same problems I thought I'd left behind while simultaneously getting nauseous in class when I remembered how much my tuition was. College most definitely didn't include dealing with delicate economic umbrage of this guy's ego in relation to his niece's education.

"No, that's totally okay," I said, gripping my keys tighter. I was slowly catching Ashley's second-hand embarrassment. Her uncle waved his hand at my words.

"Take home some pizza." Before I could say anything, a pizza box was shoved in my hands, Ashley standing behind the box, a defensive smile on her face, lips pulled tight against her wicked teeth.

* * *

I would drive Ashley home on random weekends and get paid in pizza. I'm not sure what her arrangement was, but I never needed to drive her back to school, only home when she needed it.

Ashley and I didn't become friends. We didn't talk on the long drives and we didn't hang out at school.

We did this for a year and I remember when I dropped her off for Winter Break I pulled up to the curb of the pizza place and she leaped out before the car stopped rolling. She started tugging the garbage bag out of the back seat, her head down and her mouth twisted shut. Her shoulders tensed and I heard a loud cracking laugh that made me flinch.

The bell above the door jingled and I heard a shout.

"Well look! It's Ashley home from college. You guys! Ashley's back from college!" again that digging tone. I had gotten out of the car to collect my pizza, when the young man who had yelled, reeled backward and threw his hands up. I recognized him as someone I kind of knew from my list of people to avoid during my teen years. He was a friend of a friend who sold weed to the Methodist youth group kids and was also on the sex offender registry.

"Who is this, Ash? Your girlfriend? They teach you how to lick pussy at that fancy college?" he put his hands in his heavy canvas work coat, so tan it was almost gold in the blue icy dusk. He looked me up and down. He was scrawny, wearing jeans smeared with grease and paint, dirt caked on his boots, and a gold chain poking out of his jacket. He had an oily side fade with zig-zags cut into it. It was a look a lot of locals called "hoodneck." Half Wu-Tang Clan, half Duck Dynasty.

"What's your problem? You don't like dick?" he grinned at me, a big wad of chew in his lip. His teeth were incongruously white and straight, making the rest of his face look of-center. Implants.

"Fuck you, Jared. Shut up," she said, trying to push past him. He grabbed the trash bag and pulled it to him, the plastic snapping as it ripped.

"Want me to throw your shit in the street? Your bull-dyke bodyguard going to do anything about it?" He moved to grab the bag tighter when her uncle came out.

"Jared are you going to deliver those pizzas to the Rotary or are you going to stand around being an asshole all night?"

Jared turned and grinned at me, spit his wad of chew at Ashley's feet, and sauntered to a van parked at the corner.

Ashley pulled the bag tighter to her, holding the ripped parts closed, her eyes large and red.

"I have an empty bin," I said, opening the door and pulling out a sterilite bin with a snap lid. The car was packed tight with all the stuff I was taking home during the break. I thought it was weird that Ashley only had the one trash bag. She let me take the bag from her and dump it into the bin. I snapped the lid closed and handed it to her.

"I'm sorry Jared called you a lesbian," she said quietly. She thought I was upset that Jared called me gay, not at the fact that Jared was an aggressive yokel fuck whose time outside of a prison cell could be measured in seconds.

"Take the bin."

"Come get your pizza," she replied.

I held the door open for her and she sidled in past me to the back room where she stashed her stuff. Her grandmother waved me over. She was sitting in a corner of the pizza place, wrapping silverware in paper napkins. She'd lick her thumb heavily and then peel the napkins apart before wrapping them around the spotty silverware. A dirty oxygen tank sat hissing faintly at her feet, the canula that looped around her ears was a deep tan from the nicotine stains going into her nostrils.

"Merry Christmas," she patted my arm wetly, a string of saliva trailing from her thumb and soaking into the sleeve of my sweatshirt. "Thanks for taking care of my girl. And don't mind that boy. Jared's an angry little shit, takes after his daddy," she sighed deeply. "My girl's such a great artist. The pictures she draws, she's so talented. That's how she got the scholarship to that big school, you know. She works hard at what she wants and I want it for her but...I don't know. That place is changing her. This is probably for the best. You know how it is," she patted my arm again.

This conversation or something like it would happen every time I came in, one of her family members leading the head-shaking charge of apologetically explaining to me why Ashley was in college. Sean had just returned from Iraq, so that somehow absolved me of the sin of being a liberal college twat.

* * *

After a short holiday break, I went back for the mini-winter semester called January term, or "J-term." J-term classes were slow and sleepy. You only had classes four days a week and you only took one class. I wanted to take Physics of Everyday Objects so I wouldn't have to take an actual math class but it was full. I ended up taking glassblowing because basket weaving is for pussies who are afraid of burning themselves. During the class I made a bunch of weird heavy things I gave away as paperweights and a squat vase speckled with glittery contrasting primary colors so mashed together and hideous Sean's pet name for it is "Clown Puke." It was heavy and ostentatious and of course I still have it.

I hadn't spent a lot of time in the arts building, having begun to eschew artistic people as unrealistic assholes who don't know what hardship was. I was wandering the hallways when a painting made me stop. The student work in the gallery ranged from Okayish to Fuck You Dad, Here's a Painting That's Just My Vulva Stamped in Different Colors Across a Huge Canvas, to Obviously I Am Disturbed Because Look At My Scary Scary Sculpture Made out Of Broken Dolls and Rusty Razors.

One painting made me pause and look at it longer than the others. It stuck out because most of the canvases were unnecessarily big, this one was the only 8x10 hanging in the gallery. It was a close up of a barred owl, just the face and the eyes and the tip of a wing. It took me a minute to realize it wasn't a photograph but a painting. The artist's signature stood out in a shockingly blue scribble at the bottom corner.

One of the senior workshop assistants loomed over me. "You like that? Ashley Houghtailing. That kid is fucking gifted. She dropped out last semester. Goddamn shame. Went home to take care of her grandmother."

Ashley quit school and I hadn't even noticed. When I drove her home for the end of the semester, it was for the last time. She still had just the same two large trash bags she took with her every time. It never occurred to me that it was all she had in the world. I thought of her, of each time we drove together, how she'd curl into a ball the closer we got to Roscoe, how her eyes would glaze over even harder. I realized with a deep plummeting emptiness that she never brought a sketchbook with her, not even once.

I could wrap this up and say that I touched the paint lightly and felt the snap and thrum of an owl's wing in my chest as I breathed in response "She's not gifted, she's a gift" but people who write bullshit like that want to make other people into dolls and the world their dollhouse where everything is meaningful and fraught and emotional and beautiful for them and them only.

Ashley is so much more and so much less than that. She was another smart rural kid with immense talent who had no support at home. As much as I wanted to shake her and scream in her face to leave everybody else's bullshit behind and focus on herself I knew it would be a lie. The idea of home weighed heavily on me while I was at school: my grandmother's failing health, my parent's divorce, and my own medical problems were a heavy weight in the small boat that carried me.

My parents were drop dead proud and supportive at seeing me go to college, and I felt guilty at the idea that I was too rattled to do it right. As I got older I had begun to look to the other adults in my life for support and approval. My parents were crazily supportive, but the other adults in my life seemed to notice I was faltering and took a lot of joy in it. I felt the same way Ashley did, the hollow guilt of going home, of showing up somehow unchanged and different at the same time and yet still not good enough. I smiled the same affable smiles over the barbed comments made by people close to me and just out of earshot of my parents "Can you say 'do you want fries with that' in Latin yet?" or "Megan's just better than everybody now, you know." I still had one foot in that world, a world that felt solid, no matter how bleak, and nobody would have blamed me for giving up.

College became less a dream and more something I resigned myself to so I could stay on my mother's health insurance. I didn't actually want to be there anymore because my being there was upsetting people I cared about and I didn't want to admit that didn't feel like I was learning anything; most of my classes involved just rereading novels I'd already read in high school, watching my debt pile up, knowing deep down that it could be fun if I just stopped punishing myself for leaving home.

I don't know where Ashley is almost thirteen years later, but I do know that Roscoe underwent a minor gentrification had has breweries and some country kitsch economy to rely on now.

A new small funky hotel was built where her uncle's pizza place was and I bitterly hope she's not changing sheets there.

And maybe she isn't.

BUT FIRST, MY SWORD

The little girl standing next to me kept disappearing every time I turned my head. Not like she ducked away and hid, but vanished like a ripple in the air over hot pavement.

This happened every fifty-three seconds. I was timing it.

She was small and sickly looking with dirty blond hair and wore a rough linen shirt and a rope belt. Her features were generic filled in shapes where a face would be. If anything, I think my brain was probably randomly going for whatever memory it could and filled in the creepy little blonde girl with the kid from cover of the Goo Goo Dolls Boy Named Goo album, which is weird because I was listening to The Decemberists on my iPod so I'm not sure how my brain inserted the Goo Goo Dolls into this hallucination.

I was hallucinating.

At work.

At a pharmacy.

I was working my way through graduate school at a call

center for a large corporate pharmacy. The building's interior was painted cheerful colors with wacky designs with kooky carpet from KidZone a la 1990. It was an abysmal place to work and the only real perk was that our prescription copays were a flat $5 for any medication imaginable.

My husband had just gotten out of the Marines and had a car payment of $360 a month, plus a bunch of credit card debt from when the USMC took away his meal benefits (yes, members of the military are charged for the food they eat. It comes out of their paycheck so let's just dispel that bullshit of three meals and a free bed. They also deducted housing from his pay and made him live in a barracks room teeming with black mold for a really long time) and he had to take out a credit card to afford food for his last six months on base.

We moved in together with a huge amount of debt between us and frighteningly few ways to pay it off. It was 2009 during the recession, and job losses per month ranged anywhere between eight hundred thousand to one hundred thousand across the country.

I got a temp job to start in the call center, then they eventually brought me on full time. It was a Fortune 500 company and every few months we watched workers from all departments walking out with boxes in their arms and coats over their shoulders. Right before Christmas one year they fired half the pharmacists. I did at least manage to get Sean a job in the warehouse, so we could carpool and save money.

My job was to sit and take calls on a dedicated line for people who had to get new prescriptions. We'd fill out a form over the phone and fax the form to their doctor. It wasn't a bad task, per se but we couldn't leave our desks unless we were going on a scheduled break. If you got up to go to the bathroom during your non-designated break time, you had to take 5 minutes off your lunch break. Since our breaks were randomly assigned and we had mandatory overtime most days, you could clock in at 8am and not have a break until 1pm, or clock in at 8 and have a break at 8:30 and not have another one until 3:30pm.

They bought us pizza once in a while so that made all the times I got a UTI from holding it all day totally worth it. They also had bullshit attendance policies that included zero sick-time and a policy that stated they didn't accept doctor's notes or medical documentation of any kind. If you missed enough time on the phone, they took it out of your vacation time at the end of the month. Maternity leave was non-existent and HR had a policy that punished the staff for discussing policies amongst each other. They also corralled us together once and threatened us with mass firing if we unionized.

But them bennies though. The medical insurance was bullshit and almost nothing was covered. Inversely, my $7,000 a month specialty injection was covered at a $5.00 copay. I was in graduate school, so yes I could be covered under my mother's insurance until I was 26 and at the time I was 25. My mom worked for the high school I graduated from and was being bounced around the secretarial pool after having been in the same department for 18 years so there was writing on the wall that she might lose her job, too. It was better to rip the bandaid off fast. I got my own insurance through Feel Better Inc. and started getting all my bases covered just in case.

I went to a new general practitioner who had obviously seen a really interesting episode of Grey's Anatomy the night before my appointment so she took me off Enbrel and declared that I needed to go to Johns Hopkins to get re-diagnosed. I asked her to help me file a disability claim and she laughed at me and told me I wasn't disabled, that I was perfectly healthy. Because sending perfectly healthy people to Johns Hopkins is a thing, I guess.

Also, she was full of shit. She took me off the Enbrel and started me on max doses of two separate antidepressants to treat what she said was just fibromyalgia. She told me it was fine to keep taking the already incredibly high daily dose of anti-seizure medication I was taking for migraines. I went from giving myself one injection a week to taking almost 16 pills a day for disorders I didn't have. I was groggy and disoriented for about a week, but according to Dr. Thompson, *perfectly healthy*.

Then the voices started. I'd be talking to a customer on the phone and then hear a voice very clearly as if a person was standing behind me.

"You're a fucking idiot." I'd whip around and almost pull my headset off, and there'd be nobody behind me. It's not like we could all get up and wander around so I was kind of concerned...ish.

My husband made sure I stayed home from work for a week, fucking up my attendance with Feel Better Inc.. He watched me like a hawk after I took a gallon of milk out of the fridge, put it on the gas burner and then turned the burner on. I walked off and got mad when he yelled about the milk being on fire. There was a part of me under all the pills that knew something was wrong, but I didn't have the energy to care. I started seeing things out of the corner of my eye; an owl sitting on our couch, pizza stuck to the window, and when I turned to look at it, it would be gone. Needless to say, it made my assignments for graduate school that much more creative when I managed to complete them and hand them in. I fell drastically behind that semester.

Within two weeks of stopping my shot, my fingers had started curling inward like claws, which would be cool if my job was living in a hut in the woods and making lost travelers answer my three questions, but it wasn't.

* * *

When I got back to work, my boss had temped me out to another department for data-entry. This wasn't uncommon and cross-training was actually kind of fun and it got me off the phone. They put me in a cubicle in a dark corner off of a hallway that nobody used, away from both data entry and the call center.

I put in my headphones and started working when the creepy little kid showed up at my elbow. I'd turn to look at her and she'd be gone. I'd face forward and all I'd see was the screen, pulsating and squiggling. I sat like that for six hours before time came back to me. I have no memory of working, only that my iPod was dead and my computer was logged out and black. I only looked at the clock to time the apparitions of the creepy little kid. I hadn't entered any of the data they gave me, but they never really checked up on anybody who did that stuff anyway.

The next day I was back at the cubicle in the corner, not hearing voices or seeing things, but under a heavy cloud of depression—All of this is worthless and I should just kill myself.

Then a knight showed up. Yes, a knight in full armor appeared just to the right of my vision, the opposite of where the creepy little kid was and told me that the church had sentenced me to death for witchcraft. That's when I knew something was very wrong.

I was quietly sobbing in my little cubicle corner when

one of the pharmacists, Patty, found me. She stopped and touched my shoulder lightly. I jumped and later she told me I had growled at her.

Through a conversation I don't even remember, she got the gist that I was deeply depressed and what medications I was taking. I also, according to Patty, was rambling about a knight, a witch, and soap voodoo dolls in the toilet. Right before I had changed treatments, I had been reading Philippa Gregory's *The Wise Woman* and that's what my brain had managed to retain, along with the cover of the Goo Goo Doll's First album.

"Honestly, Megan. I was seconds away from calling an ambulance," she told me later.

She sat with me for a few minutes and calmed me down. She looked up my prescription information with the company (probably a HIPAA violation but I didn't care) and called my primary care doctor, my neurologist, and my rheumatologist and told them that I was experiencing dangerous interactions including hallucinations and suicidal thoughts.

Patty gave me instructions on what to stop taking immediately and what to step down on and how. She had me hang out by her department, pretending to fax stuff so she could keep an eye on me until it was time to leave.

Sean's shift in the warehouse ended and, after a quick conference with Patty, he gave me a tight smile.

"Come on, Crazypants, let's get you home. It's going to be ok."

And somehow it was.

DAWN IS THE WORST

The man stood on the other side of the desk, holding a trash bag around his waist with two embarrassed teenagers in tow, both ducking behind the glass and taking turns giving me helpless stares.

"What do you mean 'colonoscopies aren't walk-in'?" He asked angrily.

It was a Saturday and Saturday switchboard at the hospital was generally a very easy shift. It was the middle of ski season in a big resort town so most of the work was going directly to the ER. It was supposed to be a slow day.

My useless coworker, Sarah, was behind me in the staff kitchen, laughing so hard she couldn't breathe.

The gentleman in question had entered Sarah's office only minutes before, a smile on his face and a plastic contractor's bag taped around his waist. He had a pair of sweatpants on over the garbage bag and bulges at the thighs that made me think he'd cut holes in the contractor bag and taped them to his legs to make them leak-proof. He had on an expensive Patagonia fleece and was well groomed and looked, for the most part, sane, if you ignored the Gladbag pantaloons.

"I'm here for my colonoscopy," he said, shifting on his feet. The bag made a swishing sound under his sweatpants. I hoped it was swishing.

"We don't do colonoscopies on Saturday," Sarah repeated.

Outpatient procedures were rarely scheduled on Saturdays and we were usually notified first. Our office was set up like a honeycomb: four offices open to the public, with a long hallway in the back so we could go from office to office. Even with the doors shut we could hear conversations in other offices. This one piqued my interest, so I was eavesdropping from the staff kitchen.

"No, no, you've misheard me," he said, still smiling. "I found out yesterday that colon cancer runs in my family so I'm here for the emergency colonoscopy."

"Who's your doctor?" Sarah asked.

"Oh, I'm not from here. I'm on vacation with my kids and my brother called and said that his doctor just told him that we have the gene that causes colon cancer. I'm here to have an immediate emergency colonoscopy." He gestured to his incredibly embarrassed kids (who didn't have bags around their waists,) "they're here for emergency colonoscopies as well."

"Hold on a second, I'll get my coworker to help you." Sarah's voice wavered and she didn't even make it out of the office before she started cracking up.

"I need you to handle this," she said in between gasps, shoving me further into the staff kitchen. She had her head down and was slapping her knees with each giggle. She looked up. The look on my face must have been bad because she stopped giggling.

"I'll buy you coffee," she pleaded.

I knew why she was asking; besides the fact that she was laughing hard enough to break a blood vessel, the only other thing to do was to page the nurse manager and the nurse manager on shift that day was Dawn, and Dawn wasn't good with patient escalations and usually made the problem worse before it got better. Dawn hated everybody except me for some reason.

I sighed and agreed, Sarah still giggling behind me. I rounded the corner and the patient perked up when he saw me and gave me a bright smile.

"Hello! I'm here for the free emergency colonoscopy," he said. He was oddly happy about this.

"Okay, well those are not words we generally hear so I'm going to need to call and confirm if someone can see you. Outpatient procedures like colonoscopies aren't usually walk-in," I said.

"What do you mean they're not "walk-in'? This is a life-saving, medically necessary procedure that I need! How dare you deny me care?" He put his fist on his hips and I heard a squishing noise come from the depths of his trash bag.

It's really hard to accept your place in this world as the person who has to take abuse from the guy voluntarily wearing and leaking into a makeshift diaper.

"Sir, we're not denying you care. Occasionally procedures get scheduled on the weekends and we need to confirm yours. Who told you to come here?"

"The doctor on the TV! Dr. Oz! He said that if anybody in your family is diagnosed with colon cancer to go to your nearest hospital and get screened immediately!"

Of course.

"Not everything you see on TV is real, sir."

I froze.

He froze.

I couldn't believe I said that.

His son and daughter looked at me wide-eyed; the humiliation radiating off them. The daughter almost smiled at me.

I took advantage of his silence and I paged the nurse manager. Dawn wasn't good with patients, or staff, or other nurses, or human beings in general, but she was the only person in the hospital who had the authority to make this guy go away.

She called me back almost instantly. I could hear her chewing on something with seeds; she spit every few seconds, a delicate little *pa-thoo* punctuating her words.

"You paged me?" *pa-thoo* ringing out.

The patient was still frozen in fury, staring at me with a deep dislike. Both of his kids were hunched over their phones in a desperate attempt to distance themselves from the situation. One of them looked up and took a business card off the edge of the desk, furtively took a photo of it, and put it back.

"Yeah," I eyed the man who was still angrily silent. "We have a gentleman here stating that he needs a colonoscopy because he has discovered that colon cancer runs in his family." Sarah's laugh echoed from down the hallway.

He came unfrozen with a fast, angry twitch. "That's not what I said you *idiot!*" he hissed.

"Dad. *Stop,*" came an embarrassed mumble from his son. The phone rang in my office and, still giggling, I heard Sarah answer.

Dawn was still chewing and spitting on the other line. "What doctor told him to come in?"

"Dr. Oz," I said, staring him down. He stared right back at me.

"Ughhh. *Fine.* I'll be right there."

I hung up and rubbed my temple. The phone was sticky with Sarah's make-up and I felt it smear in my hair. I looked up into his angrily expectant face.

"The nurse manager will be down in just a second to help us out." Both the kids raised their heads in alarm. The girl started texting furiously and the boy just put his head in his hands.

The man gave me a slow, shark smile. "You're lucky I don't file a formal complaint. I could do it, you know."

Silently, I handed him a pen and a clipboard with a complaint form just as Sarah came back around the corner.

"I've got a problem," she whispered.

"I'm a little *busy.*"

The gentleman sat down on the bench across from me, his bag making a problematic liquid *sploosh* sound as he moved.

"It's bad," she said, waving me into the staff kitchen. "The teenagers, one of them texted or called their mother. I don't know what's going on but the parents are divorced and the dad was supposed to take them skiing this weekend. Their mom just called me and said she doesn't give her permission for the kids to be admitted since they're under eighteen and she has primary custody. She's on hold right now and she's threatening to call the cops. She's, like, *really mad.* She's driving up here from New Jersey. She's about an hour away."

A big problem with the American HealthCare system is that it's clogged with idiots doing stuff like this on a regular basis.

"So did he *kidnap* his kids to bring them here to get colonoscopies?" I've seen weirder.

"I don't think so. They were supposed to be skiing and then this guy just decided now was a great time for a family bonding experience."

Dawn appeared from around the corner at the end of a very long hallway, taking her sweet time, munching on pomegranate and spitting the seeds into a kidney basin. She had red-pink smears of juice all over her chin and dribbles of juice down her scrubs. She had three pens squirreled into a huge auburn & white streaked top knot and two sets of glasses perched beneath it so it looked like a cross-eyed smaller version of Madame Trash Heap from Fraggle Rock sitting on her head. She was also wearing someone else's ID badge.

Dawn was the worst and I loved her for it.

"What's up?" she asked.

The two of us were huddled in the doorway of my office while the patient of the year was noisily filling out his complaint form and periodically reading what he had written out loud in a volume I could hear.

"Megan was EXTREMELY UNHELPFUL and I RECOMMEND if she's not FIRED that she UNDERGO INTENSE SENSITIVITY TRAINING."

"That him?" Dawn asked, spitting a pit into the kidney basin. Sarah started to fill her in when she put her hand up.

"I got this."

Watching Dawn work was to watch a true disaster artist thrive in chaos. She went into the office where the gentleman was writing a long missive about my failings as a human being and why I should be fired. He had flipped the complaint form over and was free-handing on the back.

He looked up with a smile at Dawn. "Oh good, are we

going to get this underway?" He gestured to his kids. "They need colonoscopies, too."

"I just need some information, sir," Dawn sat down comfortably in the chair opposite him. She turned to the teenagers, still clutching their phones in terror. "Why don't you two go and wait in the lobby and I'll come talk to you in a minute?" She smiled as they scurried out, her teeth pink and wet. Dawn turned back to the father.

"I hear your brother was diagnosed with colon cancer."

"No, no, no. I don't know what this idiot told you," he jabbed a finger in my direction, "but my brother was told by his doctor that he has a *high risk* of colon cancer." Dawn nodded, still chewing on a pomegranate.

Pa-thoo. She spit another pit into the dish where it hit the metal with a sharp little *ping* that rang out in the silence. "Did you share this information with your primary care doctor to see if it was necessary for you to get a colonoscopy?"

"I don't need to because of the free emergency screenings for colon cancer," he said, a tremble in his voice. He started breathing heavily and clutched the arm of the bench. He leaned back and closed his eyes. The color drained from his face and I noticed for the first time that under all the bullshit, he didn't look healthy.

Dawn picked a pomegranate seed off her chest and studied it for a minute making little *mmmhmmm mmmhmmm* sounds under her breath. She chewed it thoughtfully.

"What did you take to prep for this procedure?" she asked, noting the bag around his waist.

"Oh, I bought three of every stool softener and laxative I could find at Rite Aid. I took almost all of it." He said, proudly.

Pa-thoo. Ping. "I see," said Dawn, totally stone-faced. "When did you take them?"

"Last night!" he said cheerfully, like he was going to get a gold star on his medical chart under Not Full of Shit.

"Okay," Debbie said stood and plonked her kidney basin full of spit and pits on the desk and gestured for the gentleman to stand, which he did, unsteadily, as she walked him across the hallway to the emergency room clerk. "We're going to check this gentleman in for laxative overdose and dehydration," she said to the orderly standing in the hallway. The orderly deposited him in a wheelchair and the ER clerk started his paperwork. Dawn stuffed her hands in her pockets and turned around, a wide smile on her face.

Sarah was anxiously gesturing with her phone; the angry ex-wife was still on hold. Dawn took the receiver. The teenagers were sitting in the lobby now, looking annoyed and relieved at the same time as they watched their father be admitted to the emergency room. Dawn was spinning her name badge around her finger, the id card making little *tick tick tick* sounds as it clinked against her keys. Dawn didn't talk much but she wasn't a quiet person.

"Hi, no worries. Nobody is being admitted for anything. This is Dawn again. I can confirm that we don't have walk-in colonoscopy programs and that we wouldn't just do invasive procedures on minors for no reason."

Sarah and I exchanged a look. *This is Dawn again?*

"They'll be waiting for you in the on-call lounge. Just come to the switchboard and ask for Megan or Sarah and they'll get your kids for you." She hung up the phone and left.

Still twirling her badge, she waved the kids from the lobby to follow her, which they hesitantly did, as if this was a massive trick and Dawn was going to chase them around the hallway with an endoscope she had hidden under her scrubs. She pulled them along and put an arm around each of them.

"Nobody's getting probed today," she said in what I think she thought was a reassuring tone. "Why don't you come with me and I'll let you into the doctor's lounge. They have HBO and a PS4. No rectal exams. I promise."

Dawn stopped at a nondescript door and entered a code into a keypad and ushered the kids inside. She saw us staring at her and gestured angrily, a flourish of pens and tags and keys. She was reaching the end of her willingness to work with us.

"What do you want *now*?"

"This is Dawn again?" Sarah said.

"Oh, yeah. The mom called about two hours ago frantic as hell. She'd been calling hospitals all over the county trying to find her kids and her ex-husband. I guess he did something like this last time he had them for the weekend. Makes me glad my ex is still in prison. Don't page me again."

We watched her walk away, twirling her keys and whistling, her pomegranate and bowl of spit still leaking pink juice onto the blotter of Sarah's desk, and I made a note to maybe change the advertising of our free colonoscopy screenings.

THE GIRL WHO CAN HANG

I pushed my housekeeping cart down a narrow hallway that reeked of cigarette smoke, bleach, and fried asshole. A lot of the Catskill hotels were dead and rotting but a few small franchise motels were still open on Route 17 mostly as crack dens. Some how a few still saw a lot of turn over. The motel I worked at was a few steps above a crack den and many steps down from a mildly unnerving Motel 6.

We didn't have any permanent guests or squatters, but we did have "massage therapists" who rented rooms by the hour, people who were cheating on their spouses, annoyed executives in town for a conference who were definitely going to fire their secretaries for booking them at such a shit hole, and occasionally an unsuspecting family from Manhattan who had car trouble on the way to the Great Lakes. The carpets had maybe been a light yellow or beige back in the 80s, but over the years had become a sticky greenish-brown, looked dirty no matter how much they were vacuumed and still reeked after being doused with 1/2 a bottle of industrial "fresh scent" air-freshener.

I stopped at the last room at the end of the dimly lit

hallway at the back of the motel. My housekeeping partner had mysteriously disappeared sometime that morning and said the laundry room needed her help; this meant she raided the leftovers from the continental breakfast after hanging out with the laundry staff and smoking weed.

The previous eighteen rooms had been mostly ok except for the skid-marks on the towels and sheets in 218, what appeared to have been the aftermath of a pube shaving party in 221, and someone taking a shit between the box spring and the mattress in 223. I was hoping 226 was going to be easy.

I had my master key in the lock and the door half open when the stench hit me: cigars and liquor and unwashed and vigorously used mucous membranes. A man stood in front of me, naked with his balls stuck to his leg and his shriveled peen looking sideways at me. A naked woman was sprawled on the bed and before I had time to react, he grabbed a handful of towels and my unopened Vanilla Pepsi left over from lunch.

He turned around and walked back into the room, but stopped in the doorway, blocking me from getting my key. He scratched his back, missing the used condom stuck between his shoulder blades, and turned around. Raucously loud porn played from the TV over which I hear his companion snoring loudly, so in retrospect, I'm relieved I didn't have to deal with a dead hooker.

"Heyyyyyyy," he looked me up and down. "Are you hourly?"

I did the only thing I could think of, and that was to rummage around in my cart and silently hand him a bag of pretzels. He dove for the pretzels and then backed away from the card reader so I could grab my master key. The door slammed shut and locked, with me still safely in the hallway, and Condomback the Great on the other side of the door.

I left the cart where it was and went home for the day.

The absurdity of standing silently in a dark empty hallway, holding out a bag of Bachman's Pretzel sticks to a potential assailant didn't hit me until much later. It must have been quite the scene: me in my navy blue pedal pusher scrub pants purchased at the dollar store for just such an occasion and my sketcher sneakers, a fresh drama mask tattoo welted on my ankle, the hotel provided grey and white pinstriped jacket with a Peter Pan collars, earnestly holding out a bag of pretzels to a deplorable with a deflating boner. He could have grabbed my wrist and yanked me in the room. It didn't occur to me that the situation was dangerous. I was furious because I thought he was just being a disgusting asshole to waste my time; I didn't realize he was threatening me until I was driving home.

* * *

The next day the inevitable riot act was waiting for me when my boss, a tiny woman with a violently red mullet, gave me hell for leaving my cart in the hall and my final room undone. This should have been an important lesson in picking my battles but my need to be right and indignant made me bowl past the facts that Vanilla Shriveled Dick Man and Naked Sally hadn't checked out nor had they requested service. I could have lied and said they didn't want turn down anyway but I said in my charmingly sassy way that I wasn't going to clean up after anybody who whipped their dick out at me and that I can't make a bed over a sleeping hooker and that I didn't feel safe and I left.

"You didn't feel *safe? You didn't feel safe?* Honey, that's life. Get fucking used to it," she flicked her cigarette butt into the ashtray.

She sent me to clean up 226, which those two stand up Americans had left spackled with every form of body fluid known to science, adding a few new ones yet to be discovered. My housekeeping partner that day was a young mom named Courtney who worked full time at a forensic psychiatric unit as a nursing aide and picked up weekend hours at the motel. She watched me furiously plunging a condom and cigar-butt clogged toilet from the edge of the sink, unfazed by the smell and drinking a Diet Sprite.

"You gotta let this go, you know," she said from her perch on the sink.

"Let what go?"

"That safety thing. You think I haven't been yanked into a room or grabbed? You think any of the women working here have done their jobs feeling 100% safe? Put your head down, keep your cart between you and the door, and don't bitch about it. You have to be able to handle these situations. You have to be able to hang with the rest of us and not make a scene about it." She threw her empty soda at the garbage can and missed, shrugging at me as it rolled under the sink with a cheerful metallic jingle.

I thought about going to college that fall and getting a better handle on life and I promised myself nobody would threaten me or corner me or scare me into anything ever again.

This was just one of the too many incidents I could talk about and I was one of the lucky ones. It took me many years to realize that smiling blankly when a little old man told me I had a great ass or laughing off a drunk dude with his dick out or politely getting a manager for a customer who told me he wanted me to get raped and catch aids was not just the price I pay for existing in this world as a woman.

"The Customer is Always Right" has morphed over time to a toxic permission slip that forces managers to let their staff be harassed, grabbed, and stalked just because they desperately need to make a buck.

Talking about sexual assault and harassment in the workplace at the rural poverty level is daunting because it is a beast with one hundred heads, all of who are yelling "BUT LOOK HOW SHE WAS DRESSED."

The rural workplace is a treacherous minefield of conservative resentment, left-over Sunday school dogma, a deep love of money disguised as patriotism, and suspicion of anybody who uses the phrase "that's not appropriate." A lot of women in rural workplaces want so much to be the "girl who can hang" that they don't notice they're also a huge part of the problem. This cone of silence is easily accomplished with gaslighting which can reach Olympic sport levels in rural settings by just simply tapping into internalized misogyny to create the ultimate breeding ground for assault and harassment and the perfect silent victim.

It seemed like a lot of the women I worked with suffered from internalized misogyny (myself included) and were so afraid of being the uptight bitch who always made trouble that they stayed dangerously silent. Think of an office full of the women who voted for Roy Moore: too deeply ingrained in the idea that abortion is worse than molestation because they were probably victimized themselves at some point in their lives, thinking that using "whatcha got" and constantly telling their male bosses sex stories kept them on the top of the list for promotions.

I'm drastically selling a lot of the smart, driven, professional women I've worked with over the years incredibly short, but something that needs to be talked about are the women who are silent and the women who survive by becoming perpetrators themselves.

* * *

When I started working for New Dawn, it really wasn't a secret that I had what other people thought was a sweet gig. I had come a long way from the kid with the pretzels in a dingy hotel hallway; I was an administrative assistant to one of the most popular millennial men in a non-profit homeless agency at the rural border of NY and Canada. Hot damn.

Jeff was 6'2 and lanky. He had a frame that said he was the progeny of a lot of Viking raids in sweepingly green Anglo countries and a paunch that said he really liked margaritas. His bow-ties said he wanted to be considered non-threatening. Jeff worked from home on Fridays and usually finished a pitcher of margaritas by 10am, which is when he'd start emailing and texting me about priority projects that came with indecipherable instructions and anxiety-inducing deadlines.

He was friendly and well liked, his black beard and green eyes giving him a jolly appearance and he had a knack for singling out the vulnerable or shy person in the group and making them feel like the most important person in the world. He had a magnetism that made you want his approval and I bought into it hard in the beginning when he sat me down and told me how important my degree was and how he was so excited he was working with someone who had "a little education under their belt." For the first time in almost a decade, somebody was putting a value on my degree, something that only I had done for a very, very long time. Jeff had given me a lot of hope and a lot to think about when it came to maybe having a career I didn't hate. He was cool like that. Jeff was also a minister.

I mention Jeff was a minister not to knock Christianity or be an atheist edge lord. I mention Jeff's godliness because he easily could lead a cult someday without even recruiting or trying and just wake up one sunny morning in Guyana with a bunch of people following him around and not remember how he got there. He was great with large crowds but got overwhelmed a lot in private. The male staff all wanted to be his best friend and the women all wanted to take a vacation in his pants. Because apparently, I'm a sexless gnome, I was mostly just annoyed at the lack of professionalism. There are jobs where you can screw around and play grab ass. Social services aren't one of them.

Female staff talked to Jeff like they were trying to hook up with him and Jesus was the common theme. It was like talking to your middle school crush: *"Oh, you're really into baseball! Me too! I, like, totes love the Steelers"* only it was with bible stuff. Women from other departments across the county would come to our office and hang out without a reason, all laughs and smiles and when Jeff came out of his office like a friendly, sexy woodchuck emerging from his burrow, they would suddenly be all sad and helpless and ask if they could go pray with him *privately,* with a few extra buttons suddenly open. With the right music and costumes, it sounded and looked a lot like the start of a porno. The prayer sessions would usually end with a lot of giggles and everybody blushing and extra-long hugs when they left his office.

Jeff had baggage like any human being. He didn't trust me and didn't give me access to 90% of the things I needed to do my job well so a lot of the time I was flying blind. He had a temper that not a lot of other people saw and he'd get into screaming fights with me about almost anything, but most of them about how I didn't anticipate his needs enough.

Jeff wasn't easy to work for, but he was very well liked by both the staff and the administration. One of the things I was least prepared for when I started working for Jeff was that people would take our professional relationship personally and go out of their way to protect their own relationship with him.

"You always have your eye on his door, why are you watching who comes and goes? You're being jealous and possessive and weird," asked Donna, our family court liaison. It was my job to keep Jeff on schedule, and keeping unscheduled foot traffic out of his office was kind of my job.

Donna was in her late twenties, short with a round face and wiry blonde hair. The farthest thing from a Kardashian — she would brag that her boyfriend said she looked just like Kim. Donna lived precariously with her boyfriend who was fifteen years her senior who told her if she got pregnant again "without his permission" he'd punch the baby out of her stomach. She also had a Live, Laugh, Love sign above her desk and sold MLM products.

The first time I met Donna was during our staff orientation. She leaned into me and pointed to Jeff.

"I want to fuck that guy. Like, so bad. Can you believe we get that kind of eye candy?"

"He's our boss," I whispered back.

"Oh, you need to be taught a thing or two about how the world works, honey."

As I got to know Donna, she painted a picture I'm all too familiar with. A smart girl growing up in a place where girls can't be smart, drinking her way through community college because being the party girl is better than being the prude, overtly sexual and very willing to share personal experience stories at inappropriate times. Underneath it all, I saw a tenacious woman who was very smart, organized, and capable. But the only thing anybody ever valued in her was her sexuality and so it became a tool she relied on frequently. One boring Tuesday afternoon, Jeff's wife stopped by to swap cars with him. She left the keys with me, waved to Donna and me, and left.

Donna turned to me. "Did you see that? That bitch hates me. Did you see how she looked at me?" Her eyes lit up and she smirked. "If that's how it is, yes. I *will* steal your man," she muttered to the retreating figure in the parking lot.

"God, you're so *possessive*," she said when I wouldn't give her Jeff's home address.

"Why did *you* get his house key and not me?" she asked, when he gave me his house key so I could check on his pets while his kid had an emergency appendectomy.

The final straw with Donna came when we had a staffing shift and got new employees. I guess she had to figure out a way to exert her dominance without peeing on the staff members, so she somehow became the leader of the I Want to Fuck Jeff club. Her vice president was Casey, a woman who would burst into song at inappropriate times like during phone conferences or webinars or Red Cross-trainings and then watch us out of the corner of her eye to see if we would complement her singing voice. She also frequently pulled her shirt tight against her chest and asked the male staff if they thought she'd gained weight.

The day before Jeff's birthday, Donna and Casey begged me to unlock his office so they could decorate it, which was weird because neither one of them had balloons or streamers. I unlocked the door and Donna bolted to Jeff's sweater on the back of his chair. She stuffed it against her face and breathed in. She grinned at me as she lowered the sweater and I watched in horrified fascination as she rubbed it between her legs.

Casey dropped to her knees and crawled under Jeff's desk, pressing her face to the fake leather seat. She breathed in with a rapturous smile. Still, on her knees, she started to adjust the chair, frown lines appearing between her eyebrows. She stopped fiddling with the chair and leaned back with a smirk.

"There!" she said. "Perfect blowjob height!"

I'm a prude and I refuse to apologize for it. My whole life I've felt like the dowdy kid, the pudgy outsider that everyone tolerates because eventually, they'll need somebody to drive them home or fix their fuckup, to eventually be dragged to the Upsidedown and eaten by a Demogorgon. I. Am. Barb. I have always been Barb to the Nancys of the world who need a ride. But there's a difference between being an anxious stick in the mud at parties to knowing that you don't sniff your boss's fart-soaked office chair or rub his sweater on your crotch.

It occurs to me that Jeff may have been aware of this behavior, maybe not. Donna and Casey were among the many women that would slip into his office and ask him in a weak baby voice if he had time to pray with them. Donna rubbing his sweater on her crotch is just as fucked up as that naked guy keeping me from getting my key. There were a lot of things that bothered me about working at New Dawn, but the one that stood out the most was the way overtly sexual behavior by the staff was blown off as "letting off steam." When you work in human services with vulnerable populations and registered sex offenders, the last thing you want to be perceived as is playful and sexy.

I felt bad for Jeff because he was being sexually harassed, whether he knew it or not. I felt angry and trapped because even if I wasn't the target, I had to listen to it. At our yearly HR reviews, we sat down individually with someone from administration and HR and talked about our goals and things we wanted to improve on. That year's meeting also included someone from the state regulatory board. I thought of Donna twerking in a skirt to Uptown Funk with her office door open and pretending to be all embarrassed when Jeff caught her, of Casey recounting in graphic detail how she masturbated in the shower to Jeff's Facebook profile picture, and of Jeff's drunken outbursts and his fan club lining up outside his office door.

When they asked me what I wanted to change or if there was anything in the staff dynamic that could be improved on, I didn't say anything.

It was such a small staff that I knew Donna and Casey would know I'd said something. I'd watched them bully other staff members into quitting and I just didn't have the energy to fight back because I couldn't lose my health insurance and I had already defaulted on one student loan. Sean's research job had lost funding. I needed a roof over my head more than I needed to be right.

I didn't want to be the uptight bitch who ruined everything. I wanted to be the girl who could hang.

THE CREDIT OF BEING HUMAN

I checked my credit the first time in almost a decade.

Sean held my hand because apparently money issues and me are akin to a seven-year-old getting a booster shot. I can skin and gut a deer. I can give myself injections every week. I can clean up barf, and handle cat-callers. I can't handle FreeCreditReport.com without needing an emotional support animal and my blankie.

The little arrow on the credit meter was pointing in a very bad direction. There was a lot of red and if the site had been playing music there would have been a slide whistle noise with a giant mushroom cloud at the end.

Sean looked over my shoulder. "It's just your student loans. Get back on the income-based repayment."

I did, but with a sinking feeling that I was going to get arrested. I could hear sirens in my sleep, and imagined the work-camp I'd be thrown into to die while my relative with the Confederate Flag tattoo laughed maniacally.

I'm currently still not in jail and nobody has ever threatened me with it. But that doesn't mean there aren't real things that could happen to me punitively: losing my social security, getting a driver's license revoked, having my wages garnished, or potentially not being able to find a job because of bad credit.

"It's just your student loans," Sean said with a soothing voice.

"This is totally fixable."

"No, it's not," I said. "This was totally preventable."

Sean gave me the same look he always gives me when we have this conversation. The I-love-you-but-you're-being-really-dumb-right-now look.

"How was this preventable? You put me through college. You were the primary earner and kept a roof over our heads for the last six years; from the time I got out of the military to literally a year ago. When were you supposed to afford any of this?"

He was right, but don't tell him I said that. Since 2010 we've shared a car. We went ten years without cell phones, cable, or streaming services. We splurged on three things in thirteen years: Sean's drum set, our English Bulldog named Shakespeare, and a trip to the Bahamas.

"You need to give yourself some credit," he ruffled my hair and stood up.

For years I believed I was a gigantic fuck up who couldn't function. Of course, my student loans were close to defaulting again. I'm an idiot who can't get my shit together.

I followed Sean into the living room where it was obvious he just wanted to lay on the couch and watch cartoons because we're adults goddamnit.

"I should have—" I started to say.

"Should have what? Not gotten an autoimmune disease? You've got permanent damage to your organs and joints by pushing yourself to the breaking point to make sure we weren't homeless. What the fuck else were you going to do? You need to give yourself some credit and stop being so hard on yourself. You're not special. You're not the only person who makes mistakes. You are not alone in being imperfect."

You are not alone in being imperfect.

I don't listen to or remember 99% of what my husband says. But I remembered that. I thought of bullshitting this chapter and making a pull-out workbook full of a bunch of lies about how to budget and fix your finances and be debt free. Fuck if I know how to do any of that shit. And it's okay that I don't. Because it's okay to be human.

SICK ENOUGH TO WANT TO BE A WRITER

Dr. Pike leaned over me with a floppy strand of red hair falling over his concerned forehead.

"Has anyone given you anything weird to eat or drink in the days before your symptoms started showing?" he paused dramatically. "I don't want you to feel like you're ratting out someone you care about, but has anybody, maybe a family member, given you anything that tasted strange or forced you to eat or drink something before your symptoms started?"

This guy watched way too much TV.

My job that summer was as head-housekeeper on the night shift of a franchise campground based off a Hana-Barbara cartoon; Yogi Bear's Jellystone Park. From 2pm to 2am, four nights a week, I wore a ranger hat and rode a golf cart around the 10-acre campground, checking the bath-houses for used condoms stuck to the walls and gigantic-you-should-see-a-doctor sized chuds in the shower drain. I cleaned up a lot of bodily fluids that summer. People on vacation are the worst.

The paper crinkled under me, conspicuously reminding

me I had no dignity left. I was fully clothed, in a weird half sitting half lying down position so that my bloated feet could be raised up on a small platform. Dr. Pike's eyes were wet with concern. I thought the question was stupid but was relieved that I didn't have to answer any more questions about my sex life—many of the male doctors who had examined all my weird symptoms assumed there was something sinful and wrong with my lady parts or least that I was using them to do something sinful and wrong.

The idea that my mother somehow poisoned me, which is what Dr. Pike was getting at, was laughable. By the time I came home from work, my mom was asleep. By the time she came back, I was either still asleep or at work, scraping a congealed tampon out of the fabric of the pool cabana couch. Surprisingly enough, my job wallowing in the bodily fluids of rude vacationers did not raise red flags to the medical staff.

Dr. Pike was going, not so subtly, with Munchausen Syndrome (now known as Factious Disorder Imposed on the self) which is a staple of Lifetime Movies and Jodi Piccoult plots.

* * *

My parents had separated that same summer. Having lived with them my whole life up to that point, I can say without malice that their divorce wasn't a surprise nor was I opposed to the idea.

Shortly after my father moved out, I started to notice my ankles were swelling. I had spent the previous year as a Freshman at a for-profit theater conservatory, where the department head pulled me aside for a friendly chat that basically boiled down to "you're fat and ugly, please drop out of my department." After that kind of pep-talk, my eating disorder was well underway and by July I had been weighing myself every day, sometimes three or four times a day.

I hit a tipping point where I started gaining weight. Half a pound a day, two pounds a day, thirteen pounds in a week. After I gained eighteen pounds in four days and my feet swelled so badly my shoes didn't fit, we went to my childhood doctor, an Eastern European socks and sandals type who told me without any blood work that it was just the freshman 15 "a little later than normal" and that I was probably stress-eating because of the divorce. He prescribed me Metformin, a drug for Type II Diabetes because it would "curb my appetite." My mother pushed him a little and he said if I didn't feel better in a month that he'd run some labs.

By the end of July, I'd gained 27lbs. I went from 169lbs to just a little over 200.

We went back for blood work and his nurse said, "Maybe you should stay away from the fridge." She drew blood and they increased the metformin.

I was also starting to experience extreme shooting pains deep in my muscles, spasms, and painful locking of my joints. According to my doctor, it was because I was fat and depressed. He offered me a prescription for an anti-depressant and an opioid. I turned him down.

Several days later he called and asked to speak to my mother. He cheerfully informed 19-year-old me that he couldn't give me my test results because I was on my mother's insurance. He told my mother I had lupus.

"What do we do now?" she asked.

"It is what it is. If it gets worse come see me. Tell her no snacking."

And that was it.

Two days later, the skin on the top of my foot split and started weeping. My toes looked like 'Lil Smokies sausages sticking out of a broken can of biscuit dough someone left in a hot car. My mom rushed me to the newly opened urgent care two towns away.

I got stuffed in an exam room by a bored-looking orderly. The only thing that fit me were old canvas flip flops, but I had broken one trying to get it between my toes. I put my bare feet against the cold floor tiles trying to get the burning boiling sensation in them to stop. It worked a little.

A young and very pretty, not at all bloated nurse came in and suddenly stopped looking so bored when she saw my feet: giant bread loaves with tiny bloated cocktail sausages for toes with jagged red welts down the top of the foot loaf. The swelling went up to my thighs and created a ridge where the water stopped and my regular leg began. She looked like she was going to give me shit for not wearing shoes, but she just closed her mouth and pulled out a footrest so I could elevate my feet.

* * *

I left with antibiotics and a few shots of something that didn't do much and a mountain of referrals for the next day: Rheumatology, Cardiology, Endocrinology, Oncology, Immunology.

Shit got real.

Nobody asked why I was taking metformin. They all assumed it was for Type II Diabetes. Which I didn't have. This would derail my diagnosis until almost October as everybody tried to figure out what was wrong with my liver.

The next week was a whirlwind of specialists. Being

dragged along medical corridors by worried looking staff and being set up to give a long medical history to each new doctor, all of whom were male and all of whom made my mom leave the room to ask me in-depth about my sex life and if I had shoved drugs in my vagina (a doctor actually asked me that).

They grimly screened me for HIV because the infectious disease specialist got grave and stern with me when I told him I was a chambermaid. He whipped out his pen-lite and started flashing it in my eyes like I was at a shitty rave.

"Did anything splash back into your eyes?" he asked urgently, looking for weeks old microscopic poop particles swimming in my vitreous humor.

All infectious panels came back fine.

Except my liver was all fucked up. They referred me to a liver specialist who told my mother and I that I might have liver cancer.

Still, nobody asked why I was taking the metformin.

Which is why I was half sitting, half lying in Dr. Pike's office in late August, telling him my mom wasn't poisoning me. He made a face at me, the kind of condescending face older men always make at women and children.

The awkward thing about Dr. Pike was that his wife was my father's divorce lawyer. This wasn't something that we had done on purpose, it just happened simultaneously; my dad got a lawyer and I got a doctor, and they happened to be related and we had figured it out earlier in the month when my mother asked Dr. Pike what his wife did.

"Oh, she's a lawyer. Specializes in family cases," he said, shining a penlight in my eye.

"Morgan Pike?" my mom asked.

"That's her!" he said cheerfully, still blinding me with the light.

"She's my husband's divorce lawyer," my mom said. Dr. Pike froze with the light in my eye until I blinked and turned away.

From that moment on, he seemed less and less engaged in my treatment and less likely to take me seriously.

My last appointment before I was set to go back to college, he asked my mom to leave the room and started asking questions about our work schedules, how much we saw each other and if she was feeding me anything that tasted weird. What he said next made me think that we weren't really adhering to HIPAA very well at home.

"Megan, we need to talk about something uncomfortable." I'd already sworn to the guy I wasn't shoving Kratom in my happyhole so I'm not sure what else he thought we could possibly have to say to one another that was more uncomfortable than that.

"Sometimes marriages don't work out. People are unhappy together and they're better off living apart. You know that, right?"

I had no idea what he was saying and after a few minutes of concrete silence, the penny dropped. This motherfucker thought I was Haley Mills and that I was drinking drain cleaner to pull a Parent Trap. He pressed on.

"With a little positivity, everything gets easier." He smiled at me, proud of himself. I truly hope he's never had to tell a patient they're dying.

Until that moment I never expected that I had to be valid to so many people; doctors, lawyers, nurses, professors, friends, even members of my own family. Going through my diagnosis lost me a lot of friends because people thought I was lying to them. One doctor said I had a lesion on my pituitary gland. Another doctor said I didn't and that my brain CT had been misread. One doctor said I had cirrhosis. Another doctor said I had kidney disease. Another doctor said I had a brain tumor. I had none of those things.

* * *

For months, each week brought new potentially life-altering news. There was not one single answer, so when people asked what was going on, I'd tell them as honestly as I could what the last doctor said.

Some of my friends started comparing notes and decided I was making shit up for attention. Being 19 is in some ways technically shittier than being 16. You're allowed to take that new-found maturity for a spin and wouldn't you know, you just dented the fender.

Support ranged from one of my friends saying, "well, I have irritable bowel syndrome and you don't hear me complaining" to "I'm not leaving my girlfriend for you so I don't know why you're making this up," to "Jesus has a plan and maybe you should listen" to "show me your stitches so I know you're not lying." When you're 19, the concept of ride or die changes when die actually becomes an option.

My friend Regina has since pointed out that people don't react well in troubling situations. "They don't want to believe bad things can happen to you," she said over one of our many nights of bad diner food. "Yes, they care about you but they're scared. If bad things can happen to you, bad things can happen to them and they don't want to think about that."

I also lashed out and stopped contacting the people who were being kind to me. Their niceness hurt worse than being told I was lying. It was sticky and felt insincere. I convinced myself people were happy I was sick, that I wouldn't succeed. That I was one less person to compete within The Adult World ™.

During the diagnosis process we were also subjected to the dreaded armchair doctors; the people who watched TLC and Discovery Channel and decided they knew what I had. I had developed large painful lumps on the back of my hands that looked like a tennis ball cut in half. If you pressed them, they squished around. I learned these were called synovial nodules, a road sign symptom of Rheumatoid Arthritis.

Several women my mother's age told me that the hand lumps were probably pieces of my breast tissue that had slid down my arm and were now infected in my hand. According to them, this medical phenomenon was caused by running around without a bra on. None of these women had a sense of humor so I know they were 100% serious. So many women said it to me that I'm curious as to what the fuck was going on for that generation of women that made them think that you could end up with titty-mittens.

* * *

By late August, they had narrowed some things down. I was on a really strong diuretic to keep the swelling down. I maxed out at 235 pounds, and they decided to let me pee out what was actually water, not fat. I had extreme pitting edema, and it was gross. You could grab my leg and leave a handprint in it that I'd slowly watch fill back up again like a water balloon.

I had sexy old lady compression socks that I pulled on with pliers if my mom wasn't home to jam them on my feet for me. I had abandoned my job at the campground, threw my rangers hat to the wind and didn't even bother quitting in person. Things like summer jobs and the pearl-clutching fear of insulting a shitty manager at a shitty job cleaning up after kinky shitty people and not getting a good reference for my next shitty summer job didn't matter. Plus, my doctors didn't want me wallowing in feces and jizz anymore.

All my tests came back negative or only slightly elevated which was incongruous with the severity of my symptoms. Sitting in Dr. Pike's exam room, swearing that I wasn't making myself sick for attention and that my mother wasn't feeding me grounded-glass and anti-freeze sandwiches, he huffed and opened his laptop.

"Well," he said. "The last option we have is a muscle biopsy. You know that's surgery, right?" he said, as if trying to scare me into admitting tearfully that I just wanted my parents back together at all costs.

He shrugged at my silence and had my mom come back into the room as he explained scheduling the biopsy.

The muscle biopsy went fairly well except for the fact that they didn't stitch my leg shut and the medical tape holding my skin together popped off and now I have a three-inch scar that looks like a second vagina on my thigh.They also got a diagnosis. Polymyositis, which is an inflammatory autoimmune disease a lot like rheumatoid arthritis, which I also have. And fibromyalgia, which even though I have it I still don't think it's real.

I got transferred back to the rheumatologist and we went about setting up a treatment system.

"Can I go back to college? School starts soon."

I don't know why I wanted to go back, since basically the school slogan should have been "Come for the body shaming, stay for the ironic sexual assault." As a kid, I was obsessed with the idea of going to college and regardless of my physical abilities, I didn't want to stay in a town where the only jobs were retail or the prison industrial complex. I just wanted to be around a bunch of happy people who made art and talked about something that wasn't hunting season or their four-wheeler. Pill by pill, that was all slipping away.

He gave me a frank but not unkind look.

"School will always be there. This needs to get handled right now. I'm still really concerned about your liver enzymes. Why are you taking the metformin again?"

"My general practitioner put me on it like back in July because I had gained too much weight."

He pinched the bridge of his nose. "Are you diabetic? Were you ever?"

"No."

He sighed. "Stop taking it. That's what's wrong with your liver. Your liver enzymes should level out once you stop taking it."

And it did.

I started a regimen of prednisone and methotrexate, a low dose chemotherapy drug. My hair thinned out quite a bit and I'm still self-conscious and worried when my I brush my hair and see loose strands. A few months later I started on Enbrel, a once a week injection that I still give myself and that Sean reminds me to take by running around the house singing Shots by LMFAO, mostly just doing the Lil Jon part loudly until he gets the dogs all excited and barking and I'm left alone to give myself a shot that feels like I'm being stung by a bee who I've personally wronged. Without insurance, it's balls to the wall expensive.

During the diagnosis process, I limped through community college, taking mostly literature classes that I knew would be easy for me. Once we had a treatment plan in place, I applied to a private college upstate to stay on my mom's health insurance. I moved to Oneonta NY and tried to put it behind me. We knew what we were facing, so that meant it was fine. Life once more handed me an opportunity to do something with myself; be a teacher or go pre-law or even nursing school. I looked life in the face, called it a little bitch, and majored in creative writing.

At least I had a reason to go get an MFA in Creative Writing. For being under thirty, I now had a lot to write about. I figured I'd pay off the student loans with my first book...

Buy lots of copies for your friends. Seriously.

I have a lot of debt.

ACKNOWLEDGMENTS

Most importantly, a huge thank you to the CLASH family; Matthew Revert, for the amazing cover, Andrew Shaffer for the killer intro, and Christoph Paul and Leza Cantoral for saying "hey, let's publish this dork's book" and then doing it. You're all quality humans and I thank you for it.

A thank you to the people I bounced very early chapters and essays off of and some of my oldest and dearest: Regina Hartman, Shena Leone, Ilyana Sawka, the Catlin/Cohen family, Katie Serviss-Kobylenski, and Emily Curtis. Each one of you saw quality in my work and for that I will always be thankful. My life would suck without you.

A huge thank you to Allison and Lindsay for showing me how to lean the fuck in and not apologize for it.

And finally, thank you for buying this book. I am poor. Buy two books and get a free plant*!

There is no plant, I'm lying

ABOUT THE AUTHOR

Megan J. Kaleita won a sci-fi short story contest when she was 15 and got real smug about it. It's been 18 years and she's still smug about it. She has a BA from Hartwick College and an MA from Wilkes University.

Her husband is a good person who has a lot of patience. Megan has published in Luna Station Quarterly and Hello Horror, and JukePop Serials. She has $35k in student debt. This is her first book.

Follow her on Twitter & Instagram @MeganJKaleita

ALSO BY CLASH BOOKS

TRAGEDY QUEENS: STORIES INSPIRED BY LANA DEL REY & SYLVIA PLATH

Edited by Leza Cantoral

GIRL LIKE A BOMB

Autumn Christian

CENOTE CITY

Monique Quintana

99 POEMS TO CURE WHATEVER'S WRONG WITH YOU OR CREATE THE PROBLEMS YOU NEED

Sam Pink

PAPI DOESN'T LOVE ME NO MORE

Anna Suarez

ARSENAL/SIN DOCUMENTOS

Francesco Levato

I'M FROM NOWHERE

Lindsay Lerman

HEAVEN IS A PHOTOGRAPH

Christine Sloan Stoddard

NEW VERONIA

M.S. Coe

TRY NOT TO THINK BAD THOUGHTS

Art by Matthew Revert

SEQUELLAND

Jay Slayton-Joslin

JAH HILLS

Unathi Slasha

GIMME THE LOOT: STORIES INSPIRED BY NOTORIOUS B.I.G

Edited by Gabino Iglesias

THE MISADVENTURES OF A JILTED JOURNALIST

Justin Little

SPORTS CENTER POEMS

Poetry by Christoph Paul & Art by Jim Agpalza

TRASH PANDA

Leza Cantoral

GODLESS HEATHENS: CONVERSATIONS WITH ATHEISTS

Edited by Andrew J. Rausch

WE PUT THE LIT IN LITERARY

CLASH

CLASHBOOKS.COM

FOLLOW US ON TWITTER, IG & FB

@CLASHBOOKS

EMAIL~ clashmediabooks@gmail.com

Bookstores & review copy ARC's